Emerson's *Nature*

With Notes

and a Personal Response

Ron McAdow

PHP

Personal History Press
Lincoln, Massachusetts

ISBN: 978-1-7357336-9-2 (hardback)

Library of Congress Control Number: 2022943387

Acknowledgments

This project was inspired by listening to Old Manse Historical Interpreter Marybeth Kelly converse with a visiting student about Emerson's essay. That got me thinking. Thank you, Marybeth, and thank you, Len Gerwick, for allowing your landscape painting—it looks so transcendental—to grace the cover. Pre-publication readers Lawrence Buell, Robert Gross, Emily Feng, Theo Collins, Molly McAdow, Marybeth Kelly, and Betsy Stokey offered valuable suggestions and support. John Butler helped me sort philosophers and philosophy. The curiosity of young learners Eloise and Ethanael keeps me going. I am grateful to all of you.

PAGE ELEMENTS

Emerson's text is in the left column

Comment by McAdow

Key point with comment

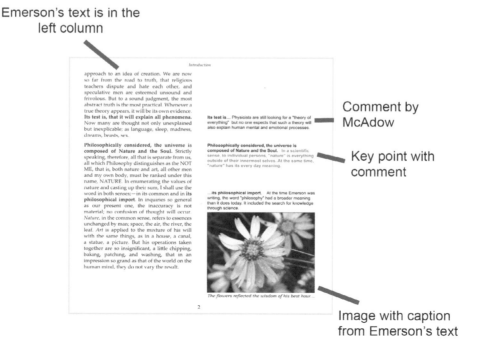

Image with caption from Emerson's text

Contents

Introduction

Our age is retrospective. It builds the sepulchres of the fathers. It writes biographies, histories, and criticism. The foregoing generations beheld God and nature face to face; we, through their eyes. **Why should not we also enjoy an original relation to the universe?** Why should not we have a poetry and philosophy of insight and not of tradition, and a religion by revelation to us, and not the history of theirs? **Embosomed for a season in nature**, whose floods of life stream around and through us, and invite us by the powers they supply, to action proportioned to nature, why should we grope among the dry bones of the past, or put the living generation into masquerade out of its faded wardrobe? **The sun shines today also.** There is more wool and flax in the fields. There are new lands, new men, new thoughts. Let us demand our own works and laws and worship.

Undoubtedly we have no questions to ask which are unanswerable. We must trust the perfection of the creation so far, as to believe that whatever curiosity the order of things has awakened in our minds, the order of things can satisfy. **Every man's condition is a solution in hieroglyphic** to those inquiries he would put. He acts it as life, before he apprehends it as truth. In like manner, nature is already, in its forms and tendencies, describing its own design. Let us interrogate the great apparition, that shines so peacefully around us. Let us inquire, to what end is nature?

All science has one aim, namely, to find a theory of nature. We have theories of races and of functions, but scarcely yet a remote

Why should not we also enjoy an original relation to the universe? Emerson urged Americans to think for themselves and to create a fresh literature based on their own experience.

Embosomed for a season in nature... Try reading this long sentence out loud. Does it sound like the lines of a poem? Emerson's use of rhythm marks some of the pleasing passages of this essay.

The sun shines today also. We, too, have light by which we may see truths for ourselves.

Every man's condition... Emerson published *Nature* in September of 1836. In March of 1833 he had written in his journal, "Every man has certain questions which always he proposes to the Eternal, and his life and fortune are so moulded as to constitute the answers, if he will read his consciousness aright." In moving this thought from his journal to his essay, Emerson expanded and clarified the idea. Hieroglyphics made a ready analogy because Jean-François Champollion had translated the Rosetta Stone a decade earlier.

approach to an idea of creation. We are now so far from the road to truth, that religious teachers dispute and hate each other, and speculative men are esteemed unsound and frivolous. But to a sound judgment, the most abstract truth is the most practical. Whenever a true theory appears, it will be its own evidence. **Its test is, that it will explain all phenomena.** Now many are thought not only unexplained but inexplicable; as language, sleep, madness, dreams, beasts, sex.

Philosophically considered, the universe is composed of Nature and the Soul. Strictly speaking, therefore, all that is separate from us, all which Philosophy distinguishes as the NOT ME, that is, both nature and art, all other men and my own body, must be ranked under this name, NATURE. In enumerating the values of nature and casting up their sum, I shall use the word in both senses;—in its common and in **its philosophical import**. In inquiries so general as our present one, the inaccuracy is not material; no confusion of thought will occur. *Nature*, in the common sense, refers to essences unchanged by man; space, the air, the river, the leaf. *Art* is applied to the mixture of his will with the same things, as in a house, a canal, a statue, a picture. But his operations taken together are so insignificant, a little chipping, baking, patching, and washing, that in an impression so grand as that of the world on the human mind, they do not vary the result.

Its test is... Physicists are still looking for a "theory of everything" but no one expects that such a theory will also explain human mental and emotional processes.

Philosophically considered, the universe is composed of Nature and the Soul. In a scientific sense, to individual persons, "nature" is everything outside of their innermost selves. At the same time, "nature" has its every day meaning.

...its philosophical import. When Emerson was writing, the word "philosophy" had a broader meaning than it does today. It included the search for knowledge through science.

The flowers reflected the wisdom of his best hour...

Chapter I

To go into solitude, a man needs to retire as much from his chamber as from society. I am not solitary whilst I read and write, though nobody is with me. But if a man would be alone, let him look at the stars. The rays that come from those heavenly worlds, will separate between him and what he touches. One might think the atmosphere was made transparent with this design, to give man, in the heavenly bodies, **the perpetual presence of the sublime.** Seen in the streets of cities, how great they are! **If the stars should appear one night in a thousand years, how would men believe and adore; and preserve for many generations the remembrance of the city of God which had been shown! But every night come out these envoys of beauty, and light the universe with their admonishing smile.**

The stars awaken a certain reverence, because though always present, they are inaccessible; but all natural objects make a kindred impression, when the mind is open to their influence. Nature never wears a mean appearance. Neither does the wisest man extort her secret, and lose his curiosity by finding out all her perfection. Nature never became a toy to a wise spirit. The flowers, the animals, the mountains, reflected the wisdom of his best hour, as much as they had delighted the simplicity of his childhood.

When we speak of nature in this manner, we have a distinct but most poetical sense in the mind. We mean the integrity of impression made by manifold natural objects. It is this which distinguishes the stick of timber of the

…the perpetual presence of the sublime. "Sublime" was an important word in the 19th century. Here it is used to mean "impressing the mind with a sense of grandeur; inspiring awe." In a subtly different usage, the awe is mixed with fear. In its simplest sense, sublime is used as a synonym of lofty.

If the stars should appear one night in a thousand years, how would men believe and adore… But every night come out these envoys of beauty, and light the universe with their admonishing smile. With the first six paragraphs of this chapter, Emerson claimed his place in American thought and literature by expressing major themes of his essay in memorable language.

The mountains reflected the wisdom of his best hour.

wood-cutter, from the tree of the poet. **The charming landscape** which I saw this morning, is indubitably made up of some twenty or thirty farms. Miller owns this field, Locke that, and Manning the woodland beyond. But none of them owns the landscape. There is a property in the horizon which no man has but he whose eye can integrate all the parts, that is, the poet. This is the best part of these men's farms, yet to this their warranty-deeds give no title.

To speak truly, few adult persons can see nature. Most persons do not see the sun. At least they have a very superficial seeing. The sun illuminates only the eye of the man, but shines into the eye and the heart of the child. **The lover of nature is he** whose inward and outward senses are still truly adjusted to each other; who has retained the spirit of infancy even into the era of manhood. His intercourse with heaven and earth, becomes part of his daily food. In the presence of nature, a wild delight runs through the man, in spite of real sorrows. Nature says,—he is my creature, and **maugre** all his impertinent griefs, he shall be glad with me. Not the sun or the summer alone, but **every hour and season yields its tribute of delight**; for every hour and change corresponds to and authorizes a different state of the mind, from breathless noon to grimmest midnight.

Nature is a setting that fits equally well a comic or a mourning piece. In good health, the air is a cordial of incredible virtue. Crossing a bare common, in snow puddles, at twilight, under a clouded sky, without having in my thoughts any occurrence of special good fortune, I have

The charming landscape... In this essay, "landscape" has its literal meaning—a visible stretch of countryside—and also becomes a symbol of the whole.

None of them owns the landscape.

The lover of nature ... Henry Thoreau was still in his teens when Emerson published *Nature*. Emerson's thinking was an important influence on his younger fellow townsman.

Maugre means "despite."

...every hour and season... Poetry was considered the highest literary art form of his day; Emerson thought of himself as both a poet and essayist. In *Nature*, he does not hesitate to mix poetic sentences with drier prose.

Nature... Linger on this paragraph! Each sentence and image is prized by those who value the thinking of the Transcendentalist writers.

enjoyed a perfect exhilaration. I am glad to the brink of fear. In the woods too, a man casts off his years, as the snake his slough, and at what period soever of life, is always a child. **In the woods, is perpetual youth.** Within these plantations of God, a decorum and sanctity reign, a perennial festival is dressed, and the guest sees not how he should tire of them in a thousand years. In the woods, **we return to reason and faith.** There I feel that nothing can befall me in life,—no disgrace, no calamity, (leaving me my eyes,) which nature cannot repair. **Standing on the bare ground,—my head bathed by the blithe air, and uplifted into infinite space,—all mean egotism vanishes. I become a transparent eye-ball; I am nothing; I see all; the currents of the Universal Being circulate through me;** I am part or particle of God. The name of the nearest friend sounds then foreign and accidental: to be brothers, to be acquaintances,—master or servant, is then a trifle and a disturbance. I am the lover of uncontained and immortal beauty. In the wilderness, I find something more dear and connate than in streets or villages. In the tranquil landscape, and especially in the distant line of the horizon, man beholds **somewhat** as beautiful as his own nature.

The greatest delight which the fields and woods minister, is the suggestion of an **occult** relation between man and the vegetable. I am not alone and unacknowledged. They nod to me, and I to them. **The waving of the boughs** in the storm, is new to me and old. It takes me by surprise, and yet is not unknown. Its effect is like that of a higher thought or a better emotion coming

In the woods is perpetual youth. For emphasis, this thought is repeated from the previous page. In 1833 Emerson had written in his journal, "When a man goes into the woods he feels like a boy without loss of wisdom."

…we return to reason and faith. European writers had divided human mental capacities into *reason* and *understanding*. *Reason* referred to our deepest intuitive power; *understanding* meant sensory or scientific knowledge, which they considered more superficial. I think today's everyday usage would reverse those labels.

Standing on the bare ground…all mean egotism vanishes;…the currents of the Universal Being circulate through me. Are there times when you feel strongly connected to the universe?

Within these plantations of God …

Somewhat means "something."
Occult means "beyond ordinary knowledge or understanding."

The waving of the boughs… Emerson imagines wind-blown branches nodding as though they acknowledged him; as though there was companionship. The human imagination provides such possibilities for our relations with the natural world.

over me, when I deemed I was thinking justly or doing right.

Yet it is certain that the power to produce this delight, does not reside in nature, but in man, or in a harmony of both. It is necessary to use these pleasures with great temperance. For, nature is not always tricked in holiday attire, but the same scene which yesterday breathed perfume and glittered as for the frolic of the nymphs, is overspread with melancholy today. **Nature always wears the colors of the spirit. To a man laboring under calamity**, the heat of his own fire hath sadness in it. Then, there is a kind of contempt of the landscape felt by him who has just lost by death a dear friend. The sky is less grand as it shuts down over less worth in the population.

Nature always wears the colors of the spirit. Our perceptions are influenced by our emotions.

To a man laboring under calamity… Emerson's first wife, Ellen, died of tuberculosis in 1831. His brother Edward died in 1834 and his brother Charles in 1836, as this essay was being completed. Emerson knew much sorrow.

Chapter II - Commodity

WHOEVER considers the final cause of the world, will discern a multitude of uses that result. They all admit of being thrown into one of the following classes; Commodity; Beauty; Language; and Discipline.

Under the general name of Commodity, I rank all those advantages which our senses owe to nature. This, of course, is a benefit which is temporary and mediate, not ultimate, like its service to the **soul**. Yet although low, it is perfect in its kind, and is the only use of nature which all men apprehend. The misery of man appears like childish petulance, when we explore the steady and prodigal provision that has been made for his support and delight on this green ball which floats him through the heavens. What angels invented these splendid ornaments, these rich conveniences, this ocean of air above, this ocean of water beneath, this firmament of earth between? this zodiac of lights, this tent of dropping clouds, this striped coat of climates, this fourfold year? Beasts, fire, water, stones, and corn serve him. The field is at once his floor, his work-yard, his play-ground, his garden, and his bed.

> More servants wait on man
> Than he'll take notice of.

Nature, in its ministry to man, is not only the material, but is also the process and the result. All the parts incessantly work into each other's hands for the profit of man. The wind sows the seed; the sun evaporates the sea; the wind blows the vapor to the field; the ice, on the other

Commodity is something of utility or value. In this brief chapter Emerson describes the ways nature is useful to human beings.

What angels invented these splendid ornaments?

... soul. The word "soul" occurs twenty-three times in this essay. Today, philosophers and psychologists rarely use "soul" to refer to an individual's essential inner being. Emerson, a minister, valued religion as the deepest field of thought. Although he inwardly rejected most religious forms and doctrines, at this stage of his life he incorporated church vocabulary and syntax into his writing. Before he wrote *Nature* he had composed nearly two hundred sermons.

More servants wait on man... This is a line from *Man* by the English poet George Herbert (1593–1633). In this essay Emerson also quotes Shakespeare, Coleridge, Goethe, Milton, and others. By including lines from distinguished, well-known authors, writers connect their work to the broader culture...and display their education.

side of the planet, condenses rain on this; the rain feeds the plant; the plant feeds the animal; and thus the endless circulations of the divine charity nourish man.

The useful arts are reproductions or new combinations by the wit of man, of the same natural benefactors. He no longer waits for favoring gales, but by means of steam, he **realizes the fable of Aeolus's bag,** and carries the two and thirty winds in the boiler of his boat. To diminish friction, **he paves the road with iron bars**, and, mounting a coach with a ship-load of men, animals, and merchandise behind him, he darts through the country, from town to town, like an eagle or a swallow through the air. By the aggregate of these aids, how is the face of the world changed, from the era of Noah to that of Napoleon! The private poor man hath cities, ships, canals, bridges, built for him. He goes to the post-office, and the human race run on his errands; to the book-shop, and the human race read and write of all that happens, for him; to the court-house, and nations repair his wrongs. He sets his house upon the road, and the human race go forth every morning, and shovel out the snow, and cut a path for him.

But there is no need of specifying particulars in this class of uses. The catalogue is endless, and the examples so obvious, that I shall leave them to the reader's reflection, with the general remark, that this mercenary benefit is one which has respect to a farther good. A man is fed, not that he may be fed, but **that he may work.**

...realizes the fable... Aeolus, master of the wind in Greek mythology, gave a sailor a bag of wind to aid his ship. Steamboats were common on America's rivers in the 1830s.

...he paves the road... The first Massachusetts railroad went into service the year before *Nature* was published. Emerson well understood the transformative importance of steam and steel. In future years, as his fame spread, railroads carried Emerson to lecture in distant cities.

On iron bars, man darts through the country...

...that he may work. We may suppose that Emerson was thinking primarily of spiritual and intellectual work—not that he denigrated other productive efforts.

Chapter III - Beauty

A nobler want of man is served by nature, namely, the love of Beauty.

The ancient Greeks called the world *kosmos*, beauty. Such is the constitution of all things, or such the plastic power of the human eye, that the primary forms, as the sky, the mountain, the tree, the animal, give us a delight in and for themselves; a pleasure arising from outline, color, motion, and grouping. This seems partly owing to the eye itself. *The eye is the best of artists.* By the mutual action of its structure and of the laws of light, perspective is produced, which integrates every mass of objects, of what character soever, into a well colored and shaded globe, so that where the particular objects are mean and unaffecting, the landscape which they compose, is round and symmetrical. And as the eye is the best composer, so light is the first of painters. There is no object so foul that intense light will not make beautiful. And the stimulus it affords to the sense, and a sort of infinitude which it hath, like space and time, make all matter gay. Even the corpse has its own beauty. But besides this general grace diffused over nature, almost all the individual forms are agreeable to the eye, as is proved by our endless imitations of some of them, as the acorn, the grape, the pine-cone, the wheat-ear, the egg, the wings and forms of most birds, the lion's claw, the serpent, the butterfly, sea-shells, flames, clouds, buds, leaves, and the forms of many trees, as the palm.

For better consideration, we may distribute the aspects of Beauty in a threefold manner.

A nobler want of man is served by nature, namely, the love of Beauty.

9

1. First, the simple perception of natural forms is a delight. The influence of the forms and actions in nature, is so needful to man, that, in its lowest functions, it seems to lie on the confines of commodity and beauty. To the body and mind which have been cramped by noxious work or company, nature is medicinal and restores their tone. The tradesman, the attorney comes out of the din and craft of the street, and sees the sky and the woods, and is a man again. In their eternal calm, he finds himself. The health of the eye seems to demand a horizon. We are never tired, so long as we can see far enough.

The health of the eye seems to demand a horizon.

But in other hours, Nature satisfies by its loveliness, and without any mixture of corporeal benefit. I see the spectacle of morning from the hill-top over against my house, from day-break to sun-rise, with emotions which an angel might share. **The long slender bars of cloud float like fishes in the sea of crimson light.** From the earth, as a shore, I look out into that silent sea. I seem to partake its rapid transformations: the active enchantment reaches my dust, and I dilate and conspire with the morning wind. How does Nature deify us with a few and cheap elements! **Give me health and a day, and I will make the pomp of emperors ridiculous.** The dawn is my Assyria; the sun-set and moon-rise **my Paphos**, and unimaginable realms of faerie; broad noon shall be my England of the senses and the understanding; the night shall be my Germany of mystic philosophy and dreams.

Not less excellent, except for our less susceptibility in the afternoon, was the charm, last evening, of a January sunset. The western

The long slender bars of cloud... Although much of this essay is abstract, here Emerson attempts to paint, in words, a visual example of nature's loveliness. In my view, he succeeds.

Give me health and a day... By switching to first person, Emerson re-captures our interest, and he excites us with the strong, compact expression of this famous sentence.

...my Paphos... Ancient Mediterranean mythology has the goddess Aphrodite dwelling at Paphos, which is on the southwest corner of Cyprus. Because Aphrodite stood for love, beauty, and passion, Emerson associates Paphos with the pleasure he receives from glorious skies.

clouds divided and subdivided themselves into pink flakes modulated with tints of unspeakable softness; and the air had so much life and sweetness, that it was a pain to come within doors. What was it that nature would say? Was there no meaning in the live repose of the valley behind the mill, and which Homer or Shakespeare could not reform for me in words? The leafless trees become spires of flame in the sunset, with the blue east for their back-ground, and the stars of the dead calices of flowers, and every withered stem and stubble rimed with frost, contribute something to **the mute music.**

The inhabitants of cities suppose that the country landscape is pleasant only half the year. I please myself with the graces of the winter scenery, and believe that we are as much touched by it as by the genial influences of summer. **To the attentive eye, each moment of the year has its own beauty,** and in the same field, it beholds, every hour, a picture which was never seen before, and which shall never be seen again. The heavens change every moment, and reflect their glory or gloom on the plains beneath. The state of the crop in the surrounding farms alters the expression of the earth from week to week. **The succession of native plants in the pastures and roadsides,** which makes the silent clock by which time tells the summer hours, will make even the divisions of the day sensible to a keen observer. The tribes of birds and insects, like the plants punctual to their time, follow each other, and the year has room for all. By water-courses, the variety is greater. In July, the blue pontederia or pickerel-weed blooms in large beds in the shallow parts of our pleasant river, and swarms

... every withered stem ...

...mute music. Is this contradiction in terms an effective way for natural beauty to be compared to artistic beauty? It reminds me of the title of a song from the 1960s: *The Sound of Silence.*

To the attentive eye each moment of the year has its own beauty... Through the active use of our senses we can enrich our lives with nature's beauty—in any season or weather.

The succession of native plants... In New England, summer wildflowers pass from jewelweed to goldenrod, and on to the purple asters of early autumn.

with yellow butterflies in continual motion. Art cannot rival this pomp of purple and gold. Indeed the river is a perpetual gala, and boasts each month a new ornament.

But this beauty of Nature which is seen and felt as beauty, is the least part. The shows of day, the dewy morning, the rainbow, mountains, orchards in blossom, stars, moonlight, shadows in still water, and the like, if too eagerly hunted, become shows merely, and mock us with their unreality. Go out of the house to see the moon, and 't is mere tinsel; it will not please as when its light shines upon your necessary journey. The beauty that shimmers in the yellow afternoons of October, who ever could clutch it? Go forth to find it, and it is gone: 't is only a mirage as you look from the windows of **diligence**.

2. The presence of a higher, namely, of the spiritual element is essential to its perfection. **The high and divine beauty which can be loved without effeminacy,** is that which is found in combination with the human will. Beauty is the mark God sets upon virtue. Every natural action is graceful. Every heroic act is also decent, and causes the place and the bystanders to shine. We are taught by great actions that the universe is the property of every individual in it. **Every rational creature has all nature for his dowry and estate. It is his, if he will.** He may divest himself of it; he may creep into a corner, and abdicate his kingdom, as most men do, but he is entitled to the world by his constitution. In proportion to the energy of his thought and will, he takes up the world into himself. "All those things for which men plough, build, or sail, obey virtue;" said **Sallust**. "The winds and

...the blue pontederia...

... diligence. This is a play on words. *Diligence* had its current meaning, but it was also another name for stagecoach.

... without effeminacy... Although today this might sound a bit sexist, we may bear in mind that Emerson respected the intellectual powers of women. His eccentric, brilliant aunt, Mary Moody Emerson, was a key figure in his development, and he knew he was indebted to his friendships with Margaret Fuller, Elizabeth Hoar, and Elizabeth Peabody.

Every rational creature... Emerson repeats his call for individuals to value their experiences in nature. The repetition, cast in this excellent turn of phrase, emphasizes a central theme of the essay.

Sallust–a Roman historian and politician, who was born in 86 BC and died in 35 BC.

waves," said **Gibbon**, "are always on the side of the ablest navigators." So are the sun and moon and all the stars of heaven. When a noble act is done,—perchance in a scene of great natural beauty; when **Leonidas** and his three hundred martyrs consume one day in dying, and the sun and moon come each and look at them once in the steep defile of Thermopylae; when **Arnold Winkelried**, in the high Alps, under the shadow of the avalanche, gathers in his side a sheaf of Austrian spears to break the line for his comrades; are not these heroes entitled to add the beauty of the scene to the beauty of the deed? When the bark of **Columbus** nears the shore of America;—before it, the beach lined with savages, fleeing out of all their huts of cane; the sea behind; and the purple mountains of the Indian Archipelago around, can we separate the man from the living picture? Does not the New World clothe his form with her palm-groves and savannas as fit drapery? Ever does natural beauty steal in like air, and envelope great actions. When **Sir Harry Vane** was dragged up the Tower-hill, sitting on a sled, to suffer death, as the champion of the English laws, one of the multitude cried out to him, "You never sate on so glorious a seat." Charles II, to intimidate the citizens of London, caused the patriot **Lord Russell** to be drawn in an open coach, through the principal streets of the city, on his way to the scaffold. "But," his biographer says, "the multitude imagined they saw liberty and virtue sitting by his side." In private places, among sordid objects, an act of truth or heroism seems at once to draw to itself the sky as its temple, the sun as its candle. **Nature stretcheth out her arms** to

Edward **Gibbon**–English historian, author of *The Decline and Fall of the Roman Empire*, published 1776 to 1788.

Leonidas–in 480 BC, Leonidas died along with his 300 Greek soldiers defending the pass of Thermopylae (480 BC) from a large army of Persian invaders.

Arnold Winkelried–According to Swiss legend, Winkelried sacrificed his life to enable a Swiss force to defeat Austrians at the Battle of Sempach in 1386.

Columbus–The famous sailor's arrival amongst the "savages" would no longer be considered an action of moral beauty, because neither Columbus nor the Europeans who followed him to America exemplified ethical heroism. They killed many of the natives, exploited many others, and imported Africans for forced labor. The relatively free political institutions that evolved in the New World we regard as a good thing, but they were based on the principles of the Enlightenment, not those of Inquisition-era Spain.

Sir Harry Vane–An English politician, briefly governor of Massachusetts, who championed religious toleration and civil liberties. During the reign of King Charles II, Vane was accused of treason and executed in 1662.

Lord Russell–Another English politician martyred by Charles II.

Nature stretcheth... The archaic verb form serves here as a warning flare that, for the rest of this paragraph, Emerson will offer a small signal-to-noise ratio, as though he needed to make this sermon a little longer. To me, this is a great essay, but I do not find equal value in every sentence.

embrace man, only let his thoughts be of equal greatness. Willingly does she follow his steps with the rose and the violet, and bend her lines of grandeur and grace to the decoration of her darling child. Only let his thoughts be of equal scope, and the frame will suit the picture. A virtuous man is in unison with her works, and makes the central figure of the visible sphere. Homer, Pindar, Socrates, Phocion, associate themselves fitly in our memory with the geography and climate of Greece. The visible heavens and earth sympathize with Jesus. And in common life, **whosoever has seen a person of powerful character and happy genius, will have remarked how easily he took all things along with him,**—the persons, the opinions, and the day, and nature became ancillary to a man.

3. There is still another aspect under which the beauty of the world may be viewed, namely, as it becomes an object of the intellect. Beside the relation of things to virtue, they have a relation to thought. The intellect searches out the absolute order of things as they stand in the mind of God, and without the colors of affection. **The intellectual and the active powers seem to succeed each other,** and the exclusive activity of the one, generates the exclusive activity of the other. There is something unfriendly in each to the other, but they are like the alternate periods of feeding and working in animals; each prepares and will be followed by the other. Therefore does beauty, which, in relation to actions, as we have seen, comes unsought, and comes because it is unsought, remain for the apprehension and

Beauty comes unsought.

...whosoever has seen a person of powerful character and happy genius, will have remarked how easily he took all things along with him. Is it true to your experience that confident, generous people affect others as a natural force?

The intellectual and the active powers... Isn't this an interesting way of stating the relationship of science to engineering, and to art?

pursuit of the intellect; and then again, in its turn, of the active power. Nothing divine dies. All good is eternally reproductive. The beauty of nature reforms itself in the mind, and not for barren contemplation, but for new creation.

All men are in some degree impressed by the face of the world; some men even to delight. This love of beauty is Taste. Others have the same love in such excess, that, not content with admiring, they seek to embody it in new forms. The creation of beauty is Art.

The production of a work of art throws a light upon the mystery of humanity. A work of art is an abstract or epitome of the world. It is the result or expression of nature, in miniature. For, although the works of nature are innumerable and all different, the result or the expression of them all is similar and single. Nature is a sea of forms radically alike and even unique. A leaf, a sun-beam, a landscape, the ocean, make an analogous impression on the mind. What is common to them all,—that perfectness and harmony, is beauty. **The standard of beauty is the entire circuit of natural forms,**—the totality of nature; which the Italians expressed by defining beauty "**il piu nell' uno**." Nothing is quite beautiful alone: nothing but is beautiful in the whole. A single object is only so far beautiful as it suggests this universal grace. The poet, the painter, the sculptor, the musician, the architect, seek each to concentrate this radiance of the world on one point, and each in his several work to satisfy the love of beauty which stimulates him to produce. Thus is Art, a nature passed through the **alembic** of man. Thus in art, does nature work through the

The works of nature are innumerable and all different.

The standard of beauty is the entire circuit of natural forms. I like to think about this notion that what looks good to us has its foundation, in the wiring of our nervous systems, from what we see in nature.

…il piu nell' uno means "the multitude in one."

An **alembic** was an apparatus for distilling a fluid.

15

will of a man filled with the beauty of her first works.

The world thus exists to the soul to satisfy the desire of beauty. This element I call an ultimate end. **No reason can be asked or given why the soul seeks beauty.** Beauty, in its largest and profoundest sense, is one expression for the universe. God is the all-fair. **Truth, and goodness, and beauty, are but different faces of the same All.** But beauty in nature is not ultimate. It is the herald of inward and eternal beauty, and is not alone a solid and satisfactory good. It must stand as a part, and not as yet the last or highest expression of the final cause of Nature.

No reason can be asked or given… How would you explain our response to beauty? Emerson associates beauty with the divine essence, to which we are inevitably drawn, or rather, from which we are inseparable.

Truth, and goodness, and beauty, are but different faces of the same All. For Emerson, the idea of God is expressed by this unity.

Chapter IV - Language

Language is a third use which Nature subserves to man. Nature is the vehicle, and threefold degree.

1. Words are signs of natural facts.

2. Particular natural facts are symbols of particular spiritual facts.

3. Nature is the symbol of spirit.

1. Words are signs of natural facts. The use of natural history is to give us aid in supernatural history: the use of the outer creation, to give us language for the beings and changes of the inward creation. **Every word which is used to express a moral or intellectual fact, if traced to its root, is found to be borrowed from some material appearance.** *Right* means *straight*; *wrong* means *twisted*. *Spirit* primarily means *wind*; *transgression*, the crossing of a *line*; *supercilious*, the *raising of the eyebrow*. We say the *heart* to express emotion, the *head* to denote thought; and *thought* and *emotion* are words borrowed from sensible things, and now appropriated to spiritual nature. Most of the process by which this transformation is made, is hidden from us in the remote time when language was framed; but the same tendency may be daily observed in children. Children and **savages** use only nouns or names of things, which they convert into verbs, and apply to analogous mental acts.

2. But this origin of all words that convey a spiritual import,—so conspicuous a fact in the history of language,—is our least debt to nature. It is not words only that are emblematic; it is

Words are signs of natural facts.

Every word...if traced to its root... The science of linguistics, or philology, was rather new, and was one of many topics Emerson learned about through reading. Language is fundamental to human beings and their culture; in this chapter Emerson discusses multiple relations of language with nature.

...savages... At the time Emerson was writing, *savage* lacked the disrespectful sound it has today. Instead, it referred to the hunter-gatherer stage of human economic culture.

things which are emblematic. Every natural fact is a symbol of some spiritual fact. Every appearance in nature corresponds to some state of the mind, and that state of the mind can only be described by presenting that natural appearance as its picture. An enraged man is a lion, a cunning man is a fox, a firm man is a rock, a learned man is a torch. A lamb is innocence; a snake is subtle spite; flowers express to us the delicate affections. Light and darkness are our familiar expression for knowledge and ignorance; and heat for love. Visible distance behind and before us, is respectively our image of memory and hope.

Who looks upon a river in a meditative hour, and is not reminded of the flux of all things? Throw a stone into the stream, and the circles that propagate themselves are the beautiful type of all influence. **Man is conscious of a universal soul within or behind his individual life, wherein, as in a firmament, the natures of Justice, Truth, Love, Freedom, arise and shine.** This universal soul, he calls Reason: it is not mine, or thine, or his, but we are its; we are its property and men. And the blue sky in which the private earth is buried, the sky with its eternal calm, and full of everlasting orbs, is the type of Reason. That which, intellectually considered, we call Reason, considered in relation to nature, we call Spirit. **Spirit is the Creator. Spirit hath life in itself.** And man in all ages and countries, embodies it in his language, as the *father*.

It is easily seen that there is nothing lucky or capricious in these analogies, but that they are

Who looks upon a river in a meditative hour, and is not reminded of the flux of all things?

Man is conscious of a universal soul within or behind his individual life— Why did Emerson place this paragraph, including a statement of his liberal theology, in the chapter about language? I am not sure. For emphasis, perhaps? To extend his thought from the end of the previous chapter? In the last sentence of the paragraph he tries, with a dubious generalization, to return to the topic of language.

Spirit is the Creator. Emerson's initial career was the Unitarian ministry. During the years he prepared this essay, he still preached regularly as a guest minister. Although he used religious forms of expression, his message was a radical departure from traditional Christianity. He firmly rejected conventional doctrines, making him a controversial figure to the religious establishment.

constant, and pervade nature. These are not the dreams of a few poets, here and there, but **man is an analogist, and studies relations in all objects.** He is placed in the center of beings, and a ray of relation passes from every other being to him. And neither can man be understood without these objects, nor these objects without man. All the facts in natural history taken by themselves, have no value, but are barren, like a single sex. But marry it to human history, and it is full of life. Whole Floras, all Linnaeus' and Buffon's volumes, are dry catalogues of facts; but the most trivial of these facts, the habit of a plant, the organs, or work, or noise of an insect, applied to the illustration of a fact in intellectual philosophy, or, in any way associated to human nature, affects us in the most lively and agreeable manner. The seed of a plant,—to what affecting analogies in the nature of man, is that little fruit made use of, in all discourse, up to the voice of Paul, who calls the human corpse a seed,—**"It is sown a natural body; it is raised a spiritual body."** The motion of the earth round its axis, and round the sun, makes the day, and the year. These are certain amounts of brute light and heat. But is there no intent of an analogy between man's life and the seasons? And do the seasons gain no grandeur or pathos from that analogy? The instincts of the ant are very unimportant, considered as the ant's; but the moment a ray of relation is seen to extend from it to man, and the little drudge is seen to be a monitor, a little body with a mighty heart, then all its habits, even that said to be recently observed, that it never sleeps, become **sublime.**

...man is an analogist... For example, the Greek philosopher Plato wrote, "The soul is like the eye: when resting upon that on which truth and being shine, the soul perceives and understands, and is radiant with intelligence; but when turned towards the twilight of becoming and perishing, then she has opinion only, and goes blinking about."

...a little body with a mighty heart...

It is sown a natural body... Emerson emphasizes the importance of natural analogies by citing this Biblical example, which is from 1 Corinthians.

... sublime. Here is that word again. Paraphrasing philosopher Emanuel Kant, the French intellectual Madame De Stael wrote, "The first effect of the sublime is to overwhelm a man, and the second to exalt him." Kant was commenting on Edmund Burke's influential treatise of 1757, *A Philosophical Enquiry into the Origin of Our Ideas of the Sublime and Beautiful*. The concept of the sublime was important in the visual arts in the 19th century—think of the haunted appearance of many of the landscape paintings.

Because of this radical correspondence between visible things and human thoughts, savages, who have only what is necessary, converse in figures. As we go back in history, language becomes more picturesque, until its infancy, when it is all poetry; or all spiritual facts are represented by natural symbols. The same symbols are found to make the original elements of all languages. It has moreover been observed, that the idioms of all languages approach each other in passages of the greatest eloquence and power. And as this is the first language, so is it the last. This immediate dependence of language upon nature, this conversion of an outward phenomenon into a type of somewhat in human life, never loses its power to affect us. It is this which gives that piquancy to **the conversation of a strong-natured farmer or back-woodsman, which all men relish.**

A man's power to connect his thought with its proper symbol, and so to utter it, depends on the simplicity of his character, that is, upon his love of truth, and his desire to communicate it without loss. The corruption of man is followed by the corruption of language. **When simplicity of character and the sovereignty of ideas is broken up by the prevalence of secondary desires, the desire of riches, of pleasure, of power, and of praise,—and duplicity and falsehood take place of simplicity and truth,** the power over nature as an interpreter of the will, is in a degree lost; new imagery ceases to be created, and old words are perverted to stand for things which are not; a paper currency is employed, when there is no bullion in the vaults. In due time, the fraud is manifest,

...As we go back in history, language becomes more picturesque...

...the conversation of a strong-natured farmer or back-woodsman, which all men relish. Perhaps Mark Twain read this, and knew he could make use of it, as in, "Sarah Wilkerson—good cretur, she was—everybody said that knowed her. She could heft a bar'l of flower as easy as I can flirt a flapjack." The quote is from *Roughing It.* (Note that some excellent 19th century American writers never lived in Concord, Massachusetts!)

When simplicity of character and the sovereignty of ideas is broken up... The disdain for "secondary desires" expressed here is part of the philosophy of Stoicism, with which Emerson is identified. Seneca, a Roman stoic philosopher, wrote "the place which in this universe is occupied by God is in man the place of the spirit. What matter is in the universe the body is in us." Stoics looked to philosophy as a guide to the cultivation of character—as did Emerson.

and words lose all power to stimulate the understanding or the affections. Hundreds of writers may be found in **every long-civilized nation**, who for a short time believe, and make others believe, that they see and utter truths, who do not of themselves clothe one thought in its natural garment, but who feed unconsciously on the language created by the primary writers of the country, those, namely, who hold primarily on nature.

But wise men pierce this rotten diction and fasten words again to visible things; so that picturesque language is at once a commanding certificate that he who employs it, is a man in alliance with truth and God. **The moment our discourse rises above the ground line of familiar facts, and is inflamed with passion or exalted by thought, it clothes itself in images.** A man conversing in earnest, if he watch his intellectual processes, will find that **a material image, more or less luminous, arises in his mind**, cotemporaneous with every thought, which furnishes the vestment of the thought. Hence, good writing and brilliant discourse are perpetual allegories. This imagery is spontaneous. It is the blending of experience with the present action of the mind. It is proper creation. It is the working of the Original Cause through the instruments he has already made.

These facts may suggest the advantage which the country-life possesses for a powerful mind, over the artificial and curtailed life of cities. We know more from nature than we can at will communicate. Its light flows into the mind evermore, and we forget its presence. The poet, the orator, bred in the woods, whose

...every long-civilized nation... Emerson repeats his call for fresh voices. He championed Walt Whitman, who wrote, in *Leaves of Grass*,

> *You shall no longer take things at second or third hand,*
> *nor look through the eyes of the dead,*
> *You shall not look through my eyes, either, nor take*
> *things from me,*
> *You shall listen to all sides and filter them your self.*
> *The look of the bay mare shames silliness out of me.*

The moment our discourse...is inflamed with passion or exalted by thought, it clothes itself in images. We can be sure Emerson wanted this essay to meet the test he expresses here. Do you think it does?

...a material image... Such images can be hyperbolic. For example, during a debate with Stephen Douglas, Abraham Lincoln said that one of his opponent's arguments was "as thin as the homeopathic soup that was made by boiling the shadow of a pigeon that had starved to death."

...the artificial and curtailed life of cities.

senses have been nourished by their fair and appeasing changes, year after year, without design and without heed,—shall not lose their lesson altogether, in the roar of cities or the broil of politics. Long hereafter, amidst agitation and terror in national councils,—in the hour of revolution,—these solemn images shall reappear in their morning lustre, as fit symbols and words of the thoughts which the passing events shall awaken. At the call of a noble sentiment, again the woods wave, the pines murmur, the river rolls and shines, and the cattle low upon the mountains, as he saw and heard them in his infancy. And with these forms, the spells of persuasion, the keys of power are put into his hands.

... these images shall reappear as fit symbols and words of the thoughts ...

3. We are thus assisted by natural objects in the expression of particular meanings. But how great a language to convey such peppercorn informations! Did it need such noble races of creatures, this profusion of forms, this host of orbs in heaven, to furnish man with the dictionary and grammar of his municipal speech? Whilst we use this grand cipher to expedite the affairs of our pot and kettle, we feel that we have not yet put it to its use, neither are able. We are like travelers using the cinders of a volcano to roast their eggs. Whilst we see that it always stands ready to clothe what we would say, we cannot avoid the question, whether the characters are not significant of themselves. Have mountains, and waves, and skies, no significance but what we consciously give them, when we employ them as emblems of our thoughts? The world is emblematic. Parts

Have mountains, and waves, and skies, no significance but what we give them?

of speech are metaphors, because **the whole of nature is a metaphor of the human mind.** The laws of moral nature answer to those of matter as face to face in a glass. **"The visible world and the relation of its parts, is the dial plate of the invisible."** The axioms of physics translate the laws of ethics. Thus, "the whole is greater than its part;" "reaction is equal to action;" "the smallest weight may be made to lift the greatest, the difference of weight being compensated by time;" and many the like propositions, which have an ethical as well as physical sense. These propositions have a much more extensive and universal sense when applied to human life, than when confined to technical use.

In like manner, the memorable words of history, and the proverbs of nations, consist usually of a natural fact, selected as a picture or parable of a moral truth. Thus; A rolling stone gathers no moss; A bird in the hand is worth two in the bush; A cripple in the right way, will beat a racer in the wrong; Make hay while the sun shines; 'T is hard to carry a full cup even; Vinegar is the son of wine; The last ounce broke the camel's back; Long-lived trees make roots first;—and the like. In their primary sense these are trivial facts, but we repeat them for the value of their analogical import. What is true of proverbs, is true of all fables, parables, and allegories.

This relation between the mind and matter is not fancied by some poet, but stands in the will of God, and so is free to be known by all men. It appears to men, or it does not appear. When in fortunate hours we ponder this

…the whole of nature is a metaphor of the human mind. Science says there are eighty-six billion nerve cells in the human brain. We cannot imagine that number, much less the number of possible interconnections. The natural world is extremely complex, but so is the human mind.

The visible world… Emerson quotes the Swedish scientist and theologian Emanuel Swedenborg (1688 – 1772). An example of a dial plate is a clock face, which expresses the workings of the instrument behind it.

Swedenborg was important to Emerson and the Transcendentalists. Central ideas in *Nature*, including the conception of God as the unity of power and life within all creation, are consistent with Swedenborg's teaching.

This relation between the mind and matter… Perhaps if he were expressing this idea today, he would have written, "The history of every human language gives evidence of the close relationship of nature to the mind."

miracle, the wise man doubts, if, at all other times, he is not blind and deaf;

—*"Can these things be,*
And overcome us like a summer's cloud,
Without our special wonder?"

for the universe becomes transparent, and the light of higher laws than its own, shines through it. It is the standing problem which has exercised the wonder and the study of every fine genius since the world began; from the era of the Egyptians and the Brahmins, to that of Pythagoras, of Plato, of Bacon, of Leibnitz, of Swedenborg. There sits the Sphinx at the road-side, and from age to age, as each prophet comes by, he tries his fortune at reading her riddle. There seems to be a necessity in spirit to manifest itself in material forms; and day and night, river and storm, beast and bird, acid and alkali, preexist in necessary Ideas in the mind of God, and are what they are by virtue of preceding affections, in the world of spirit. A Fact is the end or last issue of spirit. **The visible creation is the terminus or the circumference of the invisible world. "Material objects," said a French philosopher,** "are necessarily kinds of *scoriae* of the substantial thoughts of the Creator, which must always preserve an exact relation to their first origin; in other words, visible nature must have a spiritual and moral side."

This doctrine is abstruse, and though the images of "garment," "scoriae," "mirror," &c., may stimulate the fancy, we must summon the aid of subtler and more vital expositors to make it plain. **"Every scripture is to be interpreted by the same spirit which gave it forth,"**—is

Can these things be... This is from *Macbeth*. Emerson loved Shakespeare, studied his works, and lectured about his genius.

Visible nature must have a spiritual and moral side.

The visible creation is the...circumference of the invisible world. Emerson is far more concerned with the idea of a world beyond sensory perception than I am. Maybe it is partly the difference in our ages; perhaps younger people have a more intense need to believe in an underlying purpose for existence. Emerson was in his early thirties when he wrote *Nature*.

"Material objects," said a French philosopher... The philosopher quoted is Guillaume Oegger, a follower of Swedenborg. Emerson's friend Elizabeth Peabody gave him her translation of Oegger's work.

"Every scripture is to be interpreted... The source is English religious dissenter George Fox (1624-1691) a founder of the Quakers (or Friends).

the fundamental law of criticism. A life in harmony with nature, the love of truth and of virtue, will purge the eyes to understand her text. By degrees we may come to know the primitive sense of the permanent objects of nature, so that the world shall be to us an open book, and every form significant of its hidden life and final cause.

A new interest surprises us, whilst, under the view now suggested, we contemplate the fearful extent and multitude of objects; since **"every object rightly seen, unlocks a new faculty of the soul."** That which was unconscious truth, becomes, when interpreted and defined in an object, a part of the domain of knowledge, — a new weapon in the magazine of power.

... **"every object rightly seen ..."** The quotation is from Johann Wolfgang von Goethe (1749 – 1832), a German writer, scientist, and philosopher. Emerson studied Goethe and considered his brilliance on a plane with Shakespeare's. Goethe's thought was a fundamental inspiration for this essay.

Chapter V - Discipline

In view of the significance of nature, we arrive at once at a new fact, that nature is a discipline. This use of the world includes the preceding uses, as parts of itself.

Space, time, society, labor, climate, food, locomotion, the animals, the mechanical forces, give us sincerest lessons, day by day, whose meaning is unlimited. They educate both **the Understanding and the Reason**. Every property of matter is a school for the understanding,—its solidity or resistance, its inertia, its extension, its figure, its divisibility. The understanding adds, divides, combines, measures, and finds nutriment and room for its activity in this worthy scene. Meantime, Reason transfers all these lessons into its own world of thought, by perceiving the analogy that marries Matter and Mind.

1. Nature is a discipline of the understanding in intellectual truths. **Our dealing with sensible objects is a constant exercise in the necessary lessons of difference, of likeness, of order, of being and seeming, of progressive arrangement; of ascent from particular to general;** of combination to one end of manifold forces. Proportioned to the importance of the organ to be formed, is the extreme care with which its tuition is provided,—a care **pretermitted** in no single case. What tedious training, day after day, year after year, never ending, to form the common sense; what continual reproduction of annoyances, inconveniences, dilemmas; what rejoicing over us of little men; what disputing of prices, what

The meaning of **discipline** used here is "a field of study."

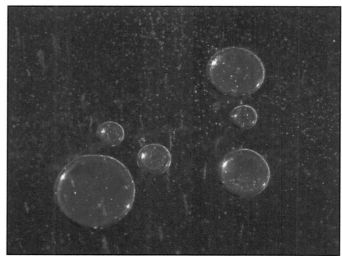

Every property of matter is a school for the understanding

...the Understanding and the Reason... Remember the note about reason vs. understanding on page 5?

Our dealing with sensible objects... On this and subsequent pages Emerson gives the study of science an unqualified endorsement.

To **pretermit** is to omit to do or mention.

reckonings of interest, —and all to form the Hand of the mind;—to instruct us that "**good thoughts are no better than good dreams, unless they be executed!**" The same good office is performed by Property and its filial systems of debt and credit. Debt, grinding debt, whose iron face the widow, the orphan, and the sons of genius fear and hate;—debt, which consumes so much time, which so cripples and disheartens a great spirit with cares that seem so base, is a preceptor whose lessons cannot be forgone, and is needed most by those who suffer from it most. Moreover, property, which has been well compared to **snow**, —"**if it fall level today, it will be blown into drifts to-morrow,**"—is the surface action of internal machinery, like the index on the face of a clock. Whilst now it is the gymnastics of the understanding, it is hiving in the foresight of the spirit, experience in profounder laws.

The whole character and fortune of the individual are affected by the least inequalities in **the culture of the understanding**; for example, in the perception of differences. Therefore is Space, and therefore Time, that man may know that things are not huddled and lumped, but sundered and individual. A bell and a plough have each their use, and neither can do the office of the other. Water is good to drink, coal to burn, wool to wear; but wool cannot be drunk, nor water spun, nor coal eaten. The wise man shows his wisdom in separation, in gradation, and his scale of creatures and of merits is as wide as nature. The foolish have no range in their scale, but suppose every man is as every other man.

Good thoughts are no better than good dreams, unless... Emerson wishes to persuade us that nature can instruct our behavior ("the Hand of the mind") as well as our understanding.

snow, "if it fall level today ... This statement is attributed to a Scottish writer, Catherine Sinclair, (1800 - 1864). In his biography of Emerson, Robert Richardson wrote, "Though Emerson was alive to the abuses of commerce...he praised the commercial spirit because it represented a more democratic form of social organization than feudalism. Emerson is virtually alone among American writers in his endorsement of the principle of commerce."

...the culture of the understanding... We might equate this phrase with intelligence—but within the word "culture," Emerson places the influences of school and family, along with inborn intellectual facility, as joint determinants of an individual's ability to evaluate his or her environment and opportunities.

Wool cannot be drunk.

What is not good they call the worst, and what is not hateful, they call the best.

In like manner, **what good heed, nature forms in us! She pardons no mistakes.** Her yea is yea, and her nay, nay.

The first steps in Agriculture, Astronomy, Zoölogy, (those first steps which the farmer, the hunter, and the sailor take,) teach that nature's dice are always loaded; that in her heaps and rubbish are concealed sure and useful results.

How calmly and genially the mind apprehends one after another the laws of physics! What noble emotions dilate the mortal as he enters into the counsels of the creation, and feels by knowledge the privilege to BE! His insight refines him. The beauty of nature shines in his own breast. Man is greater that he can see this, and the universe less, because Time and Space relations vanish as laws are known.

Here again we are impressed and even daunted by the immense Universe to be explored. "What we know, is a point to what we do not know." Open any recent journal of science, and weigh the problems suggested concerning Light, Heat, Electricity, Magnetism, Physiology, Geology, and judge whether the interest of natural science is likely to be soon exhausted.

Passing by many particulars of the discipline of nature, we must not omit to specify two.

The exercise of the Will or the lesson of power is taught in every event. From the child's successive possession of his several senses up to the hour when he saith, "Thy will be done!" he is learning the secret, that he can reduce

What good heed, nature forms... I used to tell my students that many times, in life, a good faith effort is enough—but sometimes, performance is all that counts. Will the songbird evade the hawk? Nature requires performance.

Nature's yea is yea, and her nay, nay.

under his will, not only particular events, but great classes, nay the whole series of events, and so conform all facts to his character. **Nature is thoroughly mediate. It is made to serve.** It receives the dominion of man as meekly as the ass on which the Saviour rode. It offers all its kingdoms to man as the raw material which he may mould into what is useful. Man is never weary of working it up. He forges the subtle and delicate air into wise and melodious words, and gives them wing as angels of persuasion and command. One after another, his victorious thought comes up with and reduces all things, until the world becomes, at last, only a realized will, — the double of the man.

2. Sensible objects conform to the premonitions of Reason and reflect the conscience. **All things are moral**; and in their boundless changes have an unceasing reference to spiritual nature. Therefore is nature glorious with form, color, and motion, that every globe in the remotest heaven; every chemical change from the rudest crystal up to the laws of life; every change of vegetation from the first principle of growth in the eye of a leaf, to the tropical forest and antediluvian coal-mine; every animal function from the sponge up to Hercules, shall hint or thunder to man the laws of right and wrong, and echo the Ten Commandments. Therefore is nature ever the ally of Religion: lends all her pomp and riches to the religious sentiment. Prophet and priest, David, Isaiah, Jesus, have drawn deeply from this source. This ethical character so penetrates the bone and marrow of nature, as to seem the end for which it was made. Whatever private purpose is answered by any member or part, this is its

Nature…is made to serve. In 1836, effects of the industrial age on our planet had only just begun. Even a well-informed and well-intended person could still view the "dominion of man" in a favorable light.

All things are moral – I wish he had written, "In my imagination, all things are moral." The belief expressed in this paragraph, that nature illustrates right and wrong, is not one I share. The theory of evolution emerged about twenty-five years after Emerson published this essay.

Therefore is nature glorious with form, color, and motion…

public and universal function, and is never omitted. Nothing in nature is exhausted in its first use. When a thing has served an end to the uttermost, it is wholly new for an ulterior service. In God, every end is converted into a new means. Thus the use of commodity, regarded by itself, is mean and squalid. But it is to the mind an education in the doctrine of Use, namely, that a thing is good only so far as it serves; that a conspiring of parts and efforts to the production of an end, is essential to any being. The first and gross manifestation of this truth, is our inevitable and hated training in values and wants, in corn and meat.

It has already been illustrated, that every natural process is a version of a moral sentence. The moral law lies at the center of nature and radiates to the circumference. It is the pith and marrow of every substance, every relation, and every process. All things with which we deal, preach to us. What is a farm but a mute gospel? The chaff and the wheat, weeds and plants, blight, rain, insects, sun, — it is a sacred emblem from the first furrow of spring to the last stack which the snow of winter overtakes in the fields. But the sailor, the shepherd, the miner, the merchant, in their several resorts, have each an experience precisely parallel, and leading to the same conclusion: because all organizations are radically alike. Nor can it be doubted that this moral sentiment which thus scents the air, grows in the grain, and impregnates the waters of the world, is caught by man and sinks into his soul. **The moral influence of nature upon every individual is that amount of truth which it illustrates to him.** Who can estimate this? Who can guess how much firmness the

A conspiring of parts and efforts to the production of an end, is essential to any being.

The moral influence of nature… My reaction to the past few paragraphs has been, *this is not for me*, but this sentence softens my response by situating nature's "moral influence" within a person's own reflections.

30

sea-beaten rock has taught the fisherman? how much tranquility has been reflected to man from the azure sky, over whose unspotted deeps the winds forevermore drive flocks of stormy clouds, and leave no wrinkle or stain? how much industry and providence and affection we have caught from the pantomime of brutes? What a searching preacher of self-command is the varying phenomenon of Health!

Herein is especially apprehended the unity of Nature,—the unity in variety,—which meets us everywhere. All the endless variety of things make an identical impression. Xenophanes complained in his old age, that, look where he would, all things hastened back to Unity. He was weary of seeing the same entity in the tedious variety of forms. **The fable of Proteus** has a cordial truth. A leaf, a drop, a crystal, a moment of time is related to the whole, and partakes of the perfection of the whole. **Each particle is a microcosm**, and faithfully renders the likeness of the world.

Not only resemblances exist in things whose analogy is obvious, as when we detect the type of the human hand in the flipper of the fossil saurus, but also in objects wherein there is great superficial unlikeness. Thus architecture is called "frozen music," by **De Stael** and **Goethe**. **Vitruvius** thought an architect should be a musician. "A Gothic church," said **Coleridge**, "is a petrified religion." **Michael Angelo** maintained, that, to an architect, a knowledge of anatomy is essential. In **Haydn**'s oratorios, the notes present to the imagination not only motions, as, of **the snake, the stag, and the elephant**, but colors also; as the green grass.

Who can guess how much firmness the sea-beaten rock has taught the fisherman?

The fable of Proteus... In Greek mythology, Proteus has the power of changing his shape.

Each particle... The American philosopher William James wrote, "The oneness of things, superior to their manyness, you think must also be more deeply true, must be the more real aspect of the world." (*Pragmatism*, 1907.)

Anne Louise Germaine **de Staël**-Holstein (1766 – 1817), usually refered to as Madame **de Staël**, was an influential French intellectual. **Goethe** was a German writer, **Vitruvius** a Roman architect, **Coleridge** an English poet, **Michael Angelo** a Renaissance artist, and **Haydn** an Austrian composer. Boston's Handel and Haydn Society first performed Haydn's *The Creation* while Emerson was a student at Harvard—perhaps he was in attendance.

...the snake, the stag, and the elephant – Beginning with this reference to Haydn's oratorio *The Creation*, Emerson launches a chain of associations, like a stream of consciousness, illustrating similarities among differing natural phenomena.

The law of harmonic sounds reappears in the harmonic colors. The granite is differenced in its laws only by the more or less of heat, from the river that wears it away. **The river, as it flows, resembles the air that flows over it; the air resembles the light which traverses it with more subtle currents; the light resembles the heat which rides with it through Space.** Each creature is only a modification of the other; the likeness in them is more than the difference, and their **radical** law is one and the same. A rule of one art, or a law of one organization, holds true throughout nature. So intimate is this Unity, that, it is easily seen, it lies under the undermost garment of nature, and betrays its source in Universal Spirit. For, it pervades Thought also. Every universal truth which we express in words, implies or supposes every other truth. *Omne verum vero consonat.* It is like a great circle on a sphere, comprising all possible circles; which, however, may be drawn, and comprise it, in like manner. Every such truth is the absolute **Ens** seen from one side. But it has innumerable sides.

The central Unity is still more conspicuous in actions. Words are finite organs of the infinite mind. They cannot cover the dimensions of what is in truth. They break, chop, and impoverish it. An action is the perfection and publication of thought. A right action seems to fill the eye, and to be related to all nature. "The wise man, in doing one thing, does all; or, in the

The river, as it flows, resembles the air that flows over it... Emerson chose energy and the manifestations of energy to illustrate the unity of nature, which has its source in the Universal Spirit.

We think of **radical** as meaning "drastic change" but its first definition is "of, or going to, the root or origin."

Omne verum vero consonat. – "All truth agrees with the truth." In Emerson's time, well-educated readers had studied Latin.

Ens means *existence* in the most general sense. It is not a word commonly used today. Emerson capitalized it to indicate its singularity, then remarks on its vast number of facets.

one thing he does rightly, he sees the likeness of all which is done rightly."

Words and actions are not the attributes of brute nature. They introduce us to the human form, of which all other organizations appear to be degradations. When this appears among so many that surround it, the spirit prefers it to all others. It says, 'From such as this, have I drawn joy and knowledge; in such as this, have I found and beheld myself; I will speak to it; it can speak again; it can yield me thought already formed and alive.' **In fact, the eye,—the mind,—is always accompanied by these forms, male and female; and these are incomparably the richest informations of the power and order that lie at the heart of things. Unfortunately, every one of them bears the marks as of some injury; is marred and superficially defective.** Nevertheless, far different from the deaf and dumb nature around them, these all rest like fountain-pipes on the unfathomed sea of thought and virtue whereto they alone, of all organizations, are the entrances.

It were a pleasant inquiry to follow into detail their ministry to our education, but where would it stop? We are associated in adolescent and adult life with some friends, who, like skies and waters, are coextensive with our idea; who, answering each to a certain affection of the soul, satisfy our desire on that side; whom we lack power to put at such focal distance from us, that we can mend or even analyze them. We cannot choose but love them. When much intercourse with a friend has supplied us with

…the eye,—the mind,—is always accompanied by these forms…

…these forms, male and female…Human beings exemplify the power of the universe— though each individual is flawed.

Friends, answering each to a certain affection of the soul…We cannot choose but love them.

a standard of excellence, and has increased our respect for the resources of God who thus sends a real person to outgo our ideal; when he has, moreover, become an object of thought, and, whilst his character retains all its unconscious effect, is converted in the mind into solid and sweet wisdom,—it is a sign to us that **his office is closing**, and he is commonly withdrawn from our sight in a short time.

...his office is closing... This is Waldo Emerson's subdued wail of grief for his much-loved brother Charles, who died while engaged to marry Concord native Elizabeth Hoar. Waldo and Lidian (his second wife) had moved to Concord intending to live with Charles and Elizabeth.

Chapter VI - Idealism

Thus is the unspeakable but intelligible and practicable meaning of the world conveyed to man, the immortal pupil, in every object of sense. To this one end of Discipline, all parts of nature conspire.

A noble doubt perpetually suggests itself, whether this end be not the Final Cause of the Universe; and **whether nature outwardly exists**. It is a sufficient account of that Appearance we call the World, that God will teach a human mind, and so makes it the receiver of a certain number of congruent sensations, which we call sun and moon, man and woman, house and trade. In my utter impotence to test the authenticity of the report of my senses, to know whether the impressions they make on me correspond with outlying objects, what difference does it make, whether Orion is up there in heaven, or some god paints the image in the firmament of the soul? The relations of parts and the end of the whole remaining the same, what is the difference, whether land and sea interact, and worlds revolve and intermingle without number or end, — deep yawning under deep, and galaxy balancing galaxy, throughout absolute space, — or, whether, without relations of time and space, the same appearances are inscribed in the constant faith of man?

Whether nature enjoy a substantial existence without, or is only in the apocalypse of the mind, it is alike useful and alike venerable to me. Be it what it may, it is ideal to me, so long as I cannot try the accuracy of my senses.

Today the word **idealism** means, "cherishing high or noble principles," but this chapter title refers to a philosophic usage—to doubts that the world we perceive is objectively real.

...whether nature outwardly exists. The question of whether or not matter is real or mere phenomenon was broached by a great Irish thinker, George Berkeley (1685 – 1753), whom Emerson mentions by name on page 43.

Whether nature enjoy a substantial existence without, or is only in the apocalypse of the mind, it is alike useful and alike venerable to me.

The frivolous make themselves merry with the Ideal theory, if its consequences were burlesque; as if it affected the stability of nature. It surely does not. God never jests with us, and will not compromise the end of nature, by permitting any inconsequence in its procession. Any distrust of the permanence of laws, would paralyze the faculties of man. Their permanence is sacredly respected, and his faith therein is perfect. The wheels and springs of man are all set to the hypothesis of the permanence of nature. We are not built like a ship to be tossed, but like a house to stand. It is a natural consequence of this structure, that, so long as the active powers predominate over the reflective, we resist with indignation any hint that nature is more short-lived or mutable than spirit. The broker, the wheelwright, the carpenter, the toll-man, are much displeased at the intimation.

But whilst we acquiesce entirely in the permanence of natural laws, the question of the absolute existence of nature still remains open. It is the uniform effect of culture on the human mind, not to shake our faith in the stability of particular phenomena, as of heat, water, **azote**; but to lead us to regard nature as a phenomenon, not a substance; to attribute necessary existence to spirit; to esteem nature as an accident and an effect.

To the senses and the unrenewed understanding, belongs a sort of instinctive belief in the absolute existence of nature. In their view, man and nature are indissolubly joined. Things are ultimates, and they never look beyond their sphere. The presence of Reason mars this

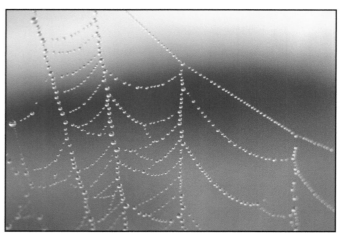

We resist with indignation any hint that nature is more short-lived or mutable than spirit.

But whilst we acquiesce entirely in the permanence of natural laws... Natural law is reliable for our practical purposes, even though we can never be certain that nature exists outside our minds.

Azote is an old name for nitrogen.

... man and nature are indissolubly joined ...

faith. The first effort of thought tends to relax this despotism of the senses, which binds us to nature as if we were a part of it, and shows us nature aloof, and, as it were, afloat. Until this higher agency intervened, the animal eye sees, with wonderful accuracy, sharp outlines and colored surfaces. When the eye of Reason opens, to outline and surface are at once added, grace and expression. These proceed from imagination and affection, and abate somewhat of the angular distinctness of objects. **If the Reason be stimulated to more earnest vision,** outlines and surfaces become transparent, and are no longer seen; causes and spirits are seen through them. The best moments of life are these delicious awakenings of the higher powers, and the reverential withdrawing of nature before its God.

Let us proceed to indicate the effects of culture.

1. Our first institution in the Ideal philosophy is a hint from nature herself. Nature is made to conspire with spirit to emancipate us. Certain mechanical changes, a small alteration in our local position apprizes us of a dualism. We are strangely affected by seeing the shore from a moving ship, from a balloon, or through the tints of an unusual sky. The least change in our point of view, gives the whole world a pictorial air. A man who seldom rides, needs only to get into a coach and traverse his own town, to turn the street into a puppet-show. The men, the women,—talking, running, bartering, fighting,—the earnest mechanic, the lounger, the beggar, the boys, the dogs, are unrealized at once, or, at least, wholly detached from all relation to the observer, and seen as apparent,

If the Reason be stimulated... These sentences, with their promise of "delicious awakenings," express a basic idea in the Transcendentalist school of thought, for which this essay was a founding document. A fuller manifesto for Transcendentalism follows on page 48.

The least change in our point of view gives the whole world a pictorial air.

not substantial beings. What new thoughts are suggested by seeing a face of country quite familiar, in the rapid movement of the rail-road car! Nay, the most wonted objects, (make a very slight change in the point of vision,) please us most. In a camera obscura, the butcher's cart, and the figure of one of our own family amuse us. So a portrait of a well-known face gratifies us. Turn the eyes upside down, by looking at the landscape through your legs, and how agreeable is the picture, though you have seen it any time these twenty years!

In these cases, by mechanical means, is suggested the difference between the observer and the spectacle,—between man and nature. Hence arises a pleasure mixed with awe; I may say, a low degree of the sublime is felt from the fact, probably, that man is hereby apprized, that, whilst the world is a spectacle, something in himself is stable.

2. In a higher manner, **the poet** communicates the same pleasure. By a few strokes he delineates, as on air, the sun, the mountain, the camp, the city, the hero, the maiden, not different from what we know them, but only lifted from the ground and afloat before the eye. He **unfixes the land and the sea, makes them revolve around the axis of his primary thought, and disposes them anew.** Possessed himself by a heroic passion, he uses matter as symbols of it. The sensual man conforms thoughts to things; the poet conforms things to his thoughts. The one esteems nature as rooted and fast; the other, as fluid, and impresses his being thereon. To him, the refractory world is ductile and flexible; he invests dust and stones

A portrait of a well-known face gratifies us.

...the poet...unfixes the land and the sea, makes them revolve around the axis of his primary thought, and disposes them anew. Creative works give us new ways to look at the world.

with humanity, and makes them the words of the Reason. The Imagination may be defined to be, the use which the Reason makes of the material world. **Shakespeare possesses the power of subordinating nature for the purposes of expression, beyond all poets.** His imperial muse tosses the creation like a bauble from hand to hand, and uses it to embody any caprice of thought that is upper-most in his mind. The remotest spaces of nature are visited, and the farthest sundered things are brought together, by a subtle spiritual connection. We are made aware that magnitude of material things is relative, and all objects shrink and expand to serve the passion of the poet. Thus, in his sonnets, the lays of birds, the scents and dyes of flowers, he finds to be the *shadow* of his beloved; time, which keeps her from him, is his *chest*; the suspicion she has awakened, is her *ornament*;

> *The ornament of beauty is Suspect,*
> *A crow which flies in heaven's sweetest air.*

His passion is not the fruit of chance; it swells, as he speaks, to a city, or a state.

> *No, it was builded far from accident;*
> *It suffers not in smiling pomp, nor falls*
> *Under the brow of thralling discontent;*
> *It fears not policy, that heretic,*
> *That works on leases of short numbered hours,*
> *But all alone stands hugely politic.*

In the strength of his constancy, the Pyramids seem to him recent and transitory. The freshness of youth and love dazzles him with its resemblance to morning.

> *Take those lips away*
> *Which so sweetly were forsworn;*

Shakespeare… In this sentence and for the rest of the paragraph, Emerson expresses his enthusiasm for the Bard. He had lectured on Shakespeare in Concord in December of 1835, the year before he published *Nature*.

Shakespeare's imperial muse tosses the creation like a bauble from hand to hand…

And those eyes,—the break of day,
Lights that do mislead the morn.

The wild beauty of this hyperbole, I may say, in passing, it would not be easy to match in literature.

This transfiguration which all material objects undergo through the passion of the poet,— this power which he exerts to dwarf the great, to magnify the small,—might be illustrated by a thousand examples from his plays. I have before me *The Tempest*, and will cite only these few lines.

> ARIEL. *The strong based promontory*
> *Have I made shake, and by the spurs plucked up*
> *The pine and cedar.*

Prospero calls for music to soothe the frantic Alonzo, and his companions:

> *A solemn air, and the best comforter*
> *To an unsettled fancy, cure thy brains*
> *Now useless, boiled within thy skull.*

Again;

> *The charm dissolves apace,*
> *And, as the morning steals upon the night,*
> *Melting the darkness, so their rising senses*
> *Begin to chase the ignorant fumes that mantle*
> *Their clearer reason.*
> *Their understanding*
> *Begins to swell: and the approaching tide*
> *Will shortly fill the reasonable shores*
> *That now lie foul and muddy.*

The perception of real affinities between events, (that is to say, of *ideal* affinities, for those only are real) enables the poet thus to make free with the most imposing forms and phenomena

This transfiguration...through the passion of the poet... Shakespeare is, for Emerson, the great example of artistic might.

...*The Tempest*... In this play, Prospero, a man with magical power, commands the services of Ariel, a genie-like supernatural being.

...as morning steals upon the night...

of the world, and to assert the predominance of the soul.

3. Whilst thus the poet animates nature with his own thoughts, he differs from the philosopher only herein, that the one proposes Beauty as his main end; the other Truth. But the philosopher, not less than the poet, postpones the apparent order and relations of things to the empire of thought. "The problem of philosophy," according to Plato, "is, for all that exists conditionally, to find a ground unconditioned and absolute." It proceeds on the faith that a law determines all phenomena, which being known, the phenomena can be predicted. That law, when in the mind, is an idea. Its beauty is infinite. **The true philosopher and the true poet are one, and a beauty, which is truth, and a truth, which is beauty, is the aim of both.** Is not the charm of one of **Plato**'s or **Aristotle**'s definitions, strictly like that of the *Antigone* of **Sophocles**? It is, in both cases, that a spiritual life has been imparted to nature; that the solid seeming block of matter has been pervaded and dissolved by a thought; that this feeble human being has penetrated the vast masses of nature with an informing soul, and recognized itself in their harmony, that is, seized their law. In physics, when this is attained, the memory disburthens itself of its cumbrous catalogues of particulars, and carries centuries of observation in a single formula.

Thus even in physics, the material is degraded before the spiritual. The astronomer, the geometer, rely on their irrefragable analysis, and disdain the results of observation. The sublime remark of **Euler** on his law of arches,

...this feeble human being has penetrated the vast masses of nature with an informing soul...

The true philosopher and the true poet are one... Although science differs from art in its priorities, both raise the power of the mind above physical reality.

Plato and **Aristotle** were Greek philosophers; **Sophocles** was a Greek playwright.

Leonhard **Euler** (1707 – 1783), was a Swiss mathematician.

"This will be found contrary to all experience, yet is true;" had already transferred nature into the mind, and left matter like an outcast corpse.

4. Intellectual science has been observed to beget invariably a doubt of the existence of matter. **Turgot** said, "He that has never doubted the existence of matter, may be assured he has no aptitude for metaphysical inquiries." It fastens the attention upon immortal necessary uncreated natures, that is, upon Ideas; and in their presence, we feel that the outward circumstance is a dream and a shade. Whilst we wait in this Olympus of gods, we think of nature as an appendix to the soul. We ascend into their region, and know that these are the thoughts of the Supreme Being. "These are they who were set up from everlasting, from the beginning, or ever the earth was. **When he prepared the heavens, they were there**; when he established the clouds above, when he strengthened the fountains of the deep. Then they were by him, as one brought up with him. Of them took he counsel."

Their influence is proportionate. As objects of science, they are accessible to few men. Yet all men are capable of being raised by piety or by passion, into their region. And no man touches these divine natures, without becoming, in some degree, himself divine. Like a new soul, they renew the body. We become physically nimble and lightsome; we tread on air; life is no longer irksome, and we think it will never be so. **No man fears age or misfortune or death, in their serene company, for he is transported out of the district of change.** Whilst we behold unveiled the nature of Justice and Truth, we

Anne Robert Jacques **Turgot** (1727–1781), was a French intellectual and official, best known as an economist.

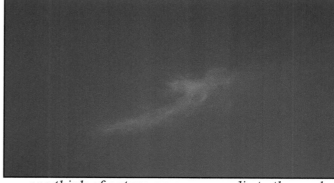

… we think of nature as an appendix to the soul.

When he prepared... Emerson has placed, in quote marks, slightly altered lines from the eighth chapter of *Proverbs*, in which Wisdom and Understanding are said to have preceded the creation of the physical world.

Their influence ... *Their* can be understood to stand for ideas, wisdom, and understanding. While reading this essay, sometimes you have to stop and search out the antecedents of Emerson's pronouns.

No man fears age or misfortune or death... A person who feels in touch with ultimate justice and truth gains a sense of immortality through the connection.

learn the difference between the absolute and the conditional or relative. We apprehend the absolute. As it were, for the first time, *we exist*. We become immortal, for we learn that time and space are relations of matter; that, with a perception of truth, or a virtuous will, they have no affinity.

5. Finally, religion and ethics, which may be fitly called *the practice of ideas, or the introduction of ideas into life*, have an analogous effect with all lower culture, in degrading nature and suggesting its dependence on spirit. Ethics and religion differ herein; that the one is the system of human duties commencing from man; the other, from God. **Religion includes the personality of God; Ethics does not. They are one to our present design. They both put nature under foot.** The first and last lesson of religion is, "The things that are seen, are temporal; the things that are unseen, are eternal." It puts an affront upon nature. It does that for the unschooled, which philosophy does for **Berkeley** and **Vyasa**. The uniform language that may be heard in the churches of the most ignorant sects, is, —"Contemn the unsubstantial shows of the world; they are vanities, dreams, shadows, unrealities; seek the realities of religion." The devotee flouts nature. Some theosophists have arrived at a certain hostility and indignation towards matter, as the **Manichean** and **Plotinus**. They distrusted in themselves any looking back to these flesh-pots of Egypt. Plotinus was ashamed of his body. In short, they might all say of matter, what Michael Angelo said of external beauty, "it is the frail and weary weed, in which God dresses the soul, which he has called into time."

Religion includes the personality of God; Ethics does not... Whether ideal life is lived in response to belief in God or in response to ethics is not of importance to this essay. In either case, ideas take precedence over nature.

George **Berkeley** (1685-1753) was an Irish philosopher associated with the theory of Idealism. **Vyasa** was a legendary sage of ancient India.

Manichaeism was a religion founded in the 3rd century AD by a prophet named Mani, who explained the cosmos as a struggle between the virtuous spiritual world of light against an evil material world of darkness. **Plotinus** (about 204– 270 AD) was an influential Greek philosopher during the period of the Roman Empire.

It appears that motion, poetry, physical and intellectual science, and religion, all tend to affect our convictions of the reality of the external world. But I own there is something ungrateful in expanding too curiously the particulars of the general proposition, that all culture tends to imbue us with idealism. I have no hostility to nature, but a child's love to it. I expand and live in the warm day like corn and melons. Let us speak her fair. I do not wish to fling stones at my beautiful mother, nor soil my gentle nest. **I only wish to indicate the true position of nature in regard to man**, wherein to establish man, all right education tends; as the ground which to attain is the object of human life, that is, of man's connection with nature. Culture inverts the vulgar views of nature, and brings the mind to call that apparent, which it uses to call real, and that real, which it uses to call visionary. Children, it is true, believe in the external world. The belief that it appears only, is an afterthought, but with culture, this faith will as surely arise on the mind as did the first.

The advantage of the ideal theory over the popular faith, is this, that it presents the world in precisely that view which is most desirable to the mind. It is, in fact, the view which Reason, both speculative and practical, that is, philosophy and virtue, take. For, seen in the light of thought, the world always is phenomenal; and virtue subordinates it to the mind. **Idealism sees the world in God.** It beholds the whole circle of persons and things, of actions and events, of country and religion, not as painfully accumulated, atom after atom, act after act, in an aged creeping Past, but as one vast picture, which God paints on the instant

... I expand and live in the warm day ...

I only wish to indicate... Because this sentence defies a clear reading, sympathetic scholars let it stand for Emerson's difficulty in wrestling with this hyper-abstract topic. Here he takes a fall.

Idealism sees the world in God. Emerson argues for thinking of God as the whole universe, because this view bears the tests of intelligence better than thinking of God in the personal terms of traditional faiths.

eternity, for the contemplation of the soul. Therefore the soul holds itself off from a too trivial and microscopic study of the universal tablet. It respects the end too much, to immerse itself in the means. It sees something more important in Christianity, than the scandals of ecclesiastical history, or the niceties of criticism; and, very incurious concerning persons or miracles, and not at all disturbed by chasms of historical evidence, it accepts from God the phenomenon, as it finds it, as the pure and awful form of religion in the world. It is not hot and passionate at the appearance of what it calls its own good or bad fortune, at the union or opposition of other persons. No man is its enemy. It accepts whatsoever befalls, as part of its lesson. It is a watcher more than a doer, and it is a doer, only that it may the better watch.

The soul accepts from God the phenomenon, as it finds it, as the pure and awful form of religion in the world.

Chapter VII - Spirit

It is essential to a true theory of nature and of man, that it should contain somewhat progressive. Uses that are exhausted or that may be, and facts that end in the statement, cannot be all that is true of this brave lodging wherein man is harbored, and wherein all his faculties find appropriate and endless exercise. And all the uses of nature admit of being summed in one, which yields the activity of man an infinite scope. **Through all its kingdoms, to the suburbs and outskirts of things, it is faithful to the cause whence it had its origin. It always speaks of Spirit.** It suggests the absolute. It is a perpetual effect. It is a great shadow pointing always to the sun behind us.

The aspect of nature is devout. Like the figure of Jesus, she stands with bended head, and hands folded upon the breast. The happiest man is he who learns from nature the lesson of worship.

Of that ineffable essence which we call Spirit, he that thinks most, will say least. We can foresee God in the coarse, and, as it were, distant phenomena of matter; but when we try to define and describe himself, both language and thought desert us, and we are as helpless as fools and savages. That essence refuses to be recorded in propositions, but when man has worshipped him intellectually, the noblest ministry of nature is to stand as the apparition of God. It is the organ through which the universal spirit speaks to the individual, and strives to lead back the individual to it.

Nature is a great shadow pointing always to the sun behind us.

Through all [nature's] kingdoms, to the suburbs and outskirts of things... Our glimpse of the divine is through nature.

Of that ineffable essence... I love this line, but it threatens to trip a writer beginning a chapter entitled "Spirit." I suppose if you plan to make your living as a lecturer, as Emerson did, you just have to keep talking.

When we consider Spirit, we see that the views already presented do not include the whole circumference of man. We must add some related thoughts.

Three problems are put by nature to the mind; **What is matter? Whence is it? and Whereto?** The first of these questions only, the ideal theory answers. **Idealism saith: matter is a phenomenon, not a substance.** Idealism acquaints us with the total disparity between the evidence of our own being, and the evidence of the world's being. The one is perfect; the other, incapable of any assurance; the mind is a part of the nature of things; **the world is a divine dream**, from which we may presently awake to the glories and certainties of day. Idealism is a hypothesis to account for nature by other principles than those of carpentry and chemistry. Yet, if it only deny the existence of matter, it does not satisfy the demands of the spirit. It leaves God out of me. It leaves me in the splendid labyrinth of my perceptions, to wander without end. Then the heart resists it, because it balks the affections in denying substantive being to men and women. Nature is so pervaded with human life, that there is something of humanity in all, and in every particular. But this theory makes nature foreign to me, and does not account for that consanguinity which we acknowledge to it.

Let it stand, then, in the present state of our knowledge, merely as a useful introductory hypothesis, serving to apprize us of the eternal distinction between the soul and the world.

What? Whence? Whereto? These questions could be restated, *What is matter? What is its source and cause? What is its purpose?*

… phenomenon… When Emerson uses the word phenomenon, he is referring to something that exists in our minds. It might or might not exist in objective reality.

…the world is a divine dream… In these paragraphs Emerson rejects the notion that our experience is mere phenomenon, because "the heart resists it."

…the splendid labyrinth of my perceptions…

But when, following the invisible steps of thought, we come to inquire, Whence is matter? and Whereto? **Many truths arise to us out of the recesses of consciousness.** We learn that the highest is present to the soul of man, that the dread universal essence, which is not wisdom, or love, or beauty, or power, but all in one, and each entirely, is that for which all things exist, and that by which they are; that spirit creates; that behind nature, throughout nature, spirit is present; one and not compound, it does not act upon us from without, that is, in space and time, but spiritually, or through ourselves: therefore, that spirit, that is, the Supreme Being, does not build up nature around us, but puts it forth through us, as the life of the tree puts forth new branches and leaves through the pores of the old. As a plant upon the earth, so a man rests upon the bosom of God; he is nourished by unfailing fountains, and draws, at his need, inexhaustible power. Who can set bounds to the possibilities of man? Once inhale the upper air, being admitted to behold the absolute natures of justice and truth, and we learn that man has access to the entire mind of the Creator, is himself the creator in the finite. This view, which admonishes me where the sources of wisdom and power lie, and points to virtue as to

> "The golden key
> Which opes the palace of eternity,"

carries upon its face the highest certificate of truth, because it animates me to create my own world through the purification of my soul.

The world proceeds from the same spirit as the body of man. It is a remoter and inferior

Many truths arise... When scholars try to summarize Transcendentalism, they could turn to this sentence, in which intuition (the recesses of consciousness) is identified as a source of wisdom. But care is required; those who were lumped together as the Transcendentalists varied in their thought.

...the highest is present to the soul of man...

The golden key... John Milton (1608 – 1674), a pre-eminent English poet, wrote "Death is the golden key that opens the palace of eternity," but Emerson substitutes *virtue* for *death*.

incarnation of God, a projection of God in the unconscious. But it differs from the body in one important respect. It is not, like that, now subjected to the human will. Its serene order is inviolable by us. It is, therefore, to us, the present expositor of the divine mind. It is a fixed point whereby we may measure our departure. As we degenerate, the contrast between us and our house is more evident. **We are as much strangers in nature, as we are aliens from God. We do not understand the notes of birds.** The fox and the deer run away from us; the bear and tiger rend us. We do not know the uses of more than a few plants, as corn and the apple, the potato and the vine. Is not the landscape, every glimpse of which hath a grandeur, a face of him? Yet this may show us what discord is between man and nature, for you cannot freely admire a noble landscape, if laborers are digging in the field hard by. The poet finds something ridiculous in his delight, until he is out of the sight of men.

Nature is the present expositor of the divine mind.

We are as much strangers in nature, as we are aliens from God. Our separation from the natural world is analgous to our separation from the divine.

Chapter VIII - Prospects

In inquiries respecting the laws of the world and the frame of things, the highest reason is always the truest. That which seems faintly possible—it is so refined, is often faint and dim because it is deepest seated in the mind among the eternal verities. Empirical science is apt to cloud the sight, and, by the very knowledge of functions and processes, to bereave the student of the manly contemplation of the whole. The savant becomes unpoetic. But **the best read naturalist who lends an entire and devout attention to truth, will see that** there remains much to learn of his relation to the world, and that it is not to be learned by any addition or subtraction or other comparison of known quantities, but **is arrived at by untaught sallies of the spirit, by a continual self-recovery, and by entire humility.** He will perceive that there are far more excellent qualities in the student than preciseness and infallibility; that a guess is often more fruitful than an indisputable affirmation, and that a dream may let us deeper into the secret of nature than a hundred concerted experiments.

For, the problems to be solved are precisely those which the physiologist and the naturalist omit to state. It is not so pertinent to man to know all the individuals of the animal kingdom, as it is to know whence and whereto is this tyrannizing unity in his constitution, which evermore separates and classifies things, endeavoring to reduce the most diverse to one form. When I behold a rich landscape, it is less to my purpose to recite correctly the order and superposition of the strata, than to know why all

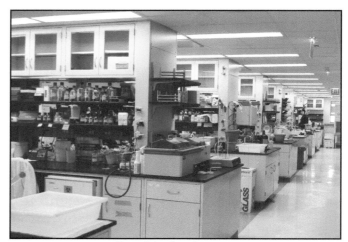

Empirical science...

...the best read naturalist who lends an entire and devout attention to truth, will see that [it] is arrived at by untaught sallies of the spirit... Science cannot teach us philosophic truth, which must be sought through **"untaught sallies of the spirit, by a continual self-recovery, and by entire humility."** Something about these last three phrases makes me take a deep, appreciative, breath.

... all the individuals of the animal kingdom ...

thought of multitude is lost in a tranquil sense of unity. I cannot greatly honor minuteness in details, so long as there is no hint to explain the relation between things and thoughts; no ray upon the metaphysics of conchology, of botany, of the arts, to show the relation of the forms of flowers, shells, animals, architecture, to the mind, and build science upon ideas. In a cabinet of natural history, we become sensible of a certain occult recognition and sympathy in regard to the most unwieldy and eccentric forms of beast, fish, and insect. The American who has been confined, in his own country, to the sight of buildings designed after foreign models, is surprised on entering York Minster or St. Peter's at Rome, by the feeling that these structures are imitations also,—faint copies of an invisible archetype. Nor has science sufficient humanity, so long as the naturalist overlooks that wonderful congruity which subsists between man and the world; of which he is lord, not because he is the most subtle inhabitant, but because he is its head and heart, and **finds something of himself in every great and small thing, in every mountain stratum, in every new law of color,** fact of astronomy, or atmospheric influence which observation or analysis lay open. A perception of this mystery inspires the muse of George Herbert, the beautiful psalmist of the seventeenth century. The following lines are part of his little poem on Man.

> *"Man is all symmetry,*
> *Full of proportions, one limb to another,*
> *And to all the world besides.*
> *Each part may call the farthest, brother;*
> *For head with foot hath private amity,*
> *And both with moons and tides.*

What is the relation of the forms of flowers and shells to the mind?

[Man] finds something of himself in every great and small thing... Every aspect of nature can be compared to something in ourselves.

... in every mountain stratum, in every law of color...

*"Nothing hath got so far
But man hath caught and kept it as his prey;
   His eyes dismount the highest star;
   He is in little all the sphere.
Herbs gladly cure our flesh, because that they
   Find their acquaintance there.*

*"For us, the winds do blow,
The earth doth rest, heaven move, and fountains
flow;
   Nothing we see, but means our good,
   As our delight, or as our treasure;
The whole is either our cupboard of food,
   Or cabinet of pleasure.*

*"The stars have us to bed:
Night draws the curtain; which the sun
withdraws.
   Music and light attend our head.
   All things unto our flesh are kind,
In their descent and being; to our mind,
   In their ascent and cause.*

*"More servants wait on man
Than he'll take notice of. In every path,
   He treads down that which doth befriend him
   When sickness makes him pale and wan.
Oh mighty love! Man is one world, and hath
   Another to attend him."*

The earth doth rest.

The perception of this class of truths makes the attraction which draws men to science, but the end is lost sight of in attention to the means. In view of this half-sight of science, we accept the sentence of Plato, that, "poetry comes nearer to vital truth than history." **Every surmise and vaticination of the mind is entitled to a certain respect,** and we learn to prefer imperfect theories, and sentences, which contain glimpses of truth, to digested systems which have no one valuable suggestion. A

Every surmise... This is another way of talking about intuition and valuing the conclusions we come to by listening to our whole selves.

wise writer will feel that the ends of study and composition are best answered by announcing undiscovered regions of thought, and so **communicating, through hope, new activity to the torpid spirit.**

I shall therefore conclude this essay with some traditions of man and nature, which **a certain poet** sang to me; and which, as they have always been in the world, and perhaps reappear to every bard, may be both history and prophecy.

'The foundations of man are not in matter, but in spirit. But the element of spirit is eternity. To it, therefore, the longest series of events, the oldest chronologies are young and recent. In the cycle of the universal man, from whom the known individuals proceed, centuries are points, and all history is but the epoch of one degradation.

'We distrust and deny inwardly our sympathy with nature. We own and disown our relation to it, by turns. We are, like **Nebuchadnezzar,** dethroned, bereft of reason, and eating grass like an ox. But who can set limits to the remedial force of spirit?

'A man is a god in ruins. When men are innocent, life shall be longer, and shall pass into the immortal, as gently as we awake from dreams. Now, the world would be insane and rabid, if these disorganizations should last for hundreds of years. It is kept in check by death and infancy. Infancy is the perpetual Messiah, which comes into the arms of fallen men, and pleads with them to return to paradise.

…communicating, through hope… Emerson sets this clear purpose for the conclusion of his essay. His intrinsically positive bent, combined with his insightfulness, gave Emerson lasting popularity.

…a certain poet… The poet referred to is Emerson himself.

The foundations of man… The part of man that concerns Emerson is the combination of intellect and emotion that we could consider a person's spiritual essence.

…Nebuchadnezzar… The reference is to a Bible story about a prophecy that this king of Babylonia would go insane for seven years, live in the fields like an animal, and eat grass.

Infancy is the perpetual Messiah…

'Man is the dwarf of himself. Once he was permeated and dissolved by spirit. He filled nature with his overflowing currents. Out from him sprang the sun and moon; from man, the sun; from woman, the moon. The laws of his mind, the periods of his actions externized themselves into day and night, into the year and the seasons. But, having made for himself this huge shell, his waters retired; he no longer fills the veins and veinlets; he is shrunk to a drop. He sees, that the structure still fits him, but fits him colossally. Say, rather, once it fitted him, now it corresponds to him from far and on high. He adores timidly his own work. Now is man the follower of the sun, and woman the follower of the moon. Yet sometimes he starts in his slumber, and wonders at himself and his house, and muses strangely at the resemblance betwixt him and it. He perceives that if his law is still paramount, if still he have elemental power, if his word is sterling yet in nature, it is not conscious power, it is not inferior but superior to his will. It is Instinct.' Thus my Orphic poet sang.

At present, man applies to nature but half his force. He works on the world with his understanding alone. He lives in it, and masters it by a penny-wisdom; and he that works most in it, is but a half-man, and whilst his arms are strong and his digestion good, his mind is imbruted, and he is a selfish savage. His relation to nature, his power over it, is through the understanding; as by manure; the economic use of fire, wind, water, and the mariner's needle; steam, coal, chemical agriculture; the repairs of the human body by the dentist and the

Man is the dwarf of himself. In this paragraph humanity is identified with the original creative force of the universe, from which humanity has shrunk to the limits we now live within.

Man's power over nature is through the use of fire, water, steam, and coal...

54

surgeon. This is such a resumption of power, as if a banished king should buy his territories inch by inch, instead of vaulting at once into his throne. Meantime, in the thick darkness, there are not wanting gleams of a better light,—occasional examples of the action of man upon nature with his entire force,—with reason as well as understanding. Such examples are; the traditions of miracles in the earliest antiquity of all nations; the history of Jesus Christ; the achievements of a principle, as in religious and political revolutions, and in the abolition of the Slave-trade; the miracles of enthusiasm, as those reported of Swedenborg, Hohenlohe, and the Shakers; many obscure and yet contested facts, now arranged under the name of Animal Magnetism; prayer; eloquence; self-healing; and the wisdom of children. **These are examples of Reason's momentary grasp of the sceptre; the exertions of a power which exists not in time or space, but an instantaneous in-streaming causing power.** The difference between the actual and the ideal force of man is happily figured by the schoolmen, in saying, that the knowledge of man is an evening knowledge, *vespertina cognitio*, but that of God is a morning knowledge, *matutina cognitio*.

The problem of restoring to the world original and eternal beauty, is solved by the redemption of the soul. The ruin or the blank, that we see when we look at nature, is in our own eye. The axis of vision is not coincident with the axis of things, and so they appear not transparent but opake. The reason why the world lacks unity, and lies broken and in heaps, is, because man is disunited with himself. He cannot be a naturalist, until he satisfies all

...the abolition of the Slave-trade...

These are examples of Reason's momentary grasp of the sceptre... which Emerson saw as possible avenues to harmony with nature and the Universal Spirit.

The problem of restoring... This statement would probably be acceptable to most Christian traditions, but Emerson's path to redemption was through intellectual and spiritual work. The difference offended some of his contemporaries, but in the long run Emerson's kindly, thoughtful tone and his moments of great eloquence made him friends and disarmed those who disagreed with him.

the demands of the spirit. Love is as much its demand, as perception. Indeed, neither can be perfect without the other. In the uttermost meaning of the words, thought is devout, and devotion is thought. Deep calls unto deep. But in actual life, the marriage is not celebrated. **There are innocent men who worship God after the tradition of their fathers, but their sense of duty has not yet extended to the use of all their faculties.** And there are patient naturalists, but they freeze their subject under the wintry light of the understanding. Is not prayer also a study of truth,—a sally of the soul into the unfound infinite? No man ever prayed heartily, without learning something. **But when a faithful thinker, resolute to detach every object from personal relations, and see it in the light of thought, shall, at the same time, kindle science with the fire of the holiest affections, then will God go forth anew into the creation.**

There are innocent men... Here is an example of Emerson distancing himself from practitioners of conventional religion, but doing so by mildly chiding them for failing to extend their thought.

...But when a faithful thinker, resolute to detach every object from personal relations, and see it in the light of thought... One way to read this is to see in it Emerson's aspiration—the path he saw before him. Or it could be his prescription for all-benefitting progress in the world.

It will not need, when the mind is prepared for study, to search for objects. The invariable mark of wisdom is to see the miraculous in the common. What is a day? What is a year? What is summer? What is woman? What is a child? What is sleep? To our blindness, these things seem unaffecting. We make fables to hide the baldness of the fact and conform it, as we say, to the higher law of the mind. But when the fact is seen under the light of an idea, the gaudy fable fades and shrivels. We behold the real higher law. To the wise, therefore, a fact is true poetry, and the most beautiful of fables. These wonders are brought to our own door. You also are a man. Man and woman, and their social life, poverty, labor, sleep, fear, fortune, are

The invariable mark of wisdom is to see the miraculous in the common.

known to you. Learn that none of these things is superficial, but that each phenomenon has its roots in the faculties and affections of the mind. Whilst the abstract question occupies your intellect, nature brings it in the concrete to be solved by your hands. It were a wise inquiry for the closet, to compare, point by point, especially at remarkable crises in life, our daily history, with the rise and progress of ideas in the mind.

So shall we come to look at the world with new eyes. It shall answer the endless inquiry of the intellect,—What is truth? and of the affections,—What is good? by yielding itself passive to the educated Will. Then shall come to pass what my poet said; 'Nature is not fixed but fluid. Spirit alters, moulds, makes it. The immobility or bruteness of nature, is the absence of spirit; to pure spirit, it is fluid, it is volatile, it is obedient. Every spirit builds itself a house; and beyond its house a world; and beyond its world, a heaven. **Know then, that the world exists for you.** For you is the phenomenon perfect. What we are, that only can we see. All that Adam had, all that Caesar could, you have and can do. Adam called his house, heaven and earth; Caesar called his house, Rome; you perhaps call yours, a cobler's trade; a hundred acres of ploughed land; or a scholar's garret. Yet line for line and point for point, your dominion is as great as theirs, though without fine names. Build, therefore, your own world. **As fast as you conform your life to the pure idea in your mind, that will unfold its great proportions.** A correspondent revolution in things will attend the influx of the spirit. So fast will disagreeable appearances,

For you is the phenomenon perfect.

Know then, that the world exists for you. Pivoting from philosophy to psychology, Emerson shifts to a pastoral voice. He wants to inspire and encourage individuals to cultivate an energetic, searching inner life.

As fast as you conform your life to the pure idea in your mind... Virtue, we are promised, will yield great inner rewards.

swine, spiders, snakes, pests, madhouses, prisons, enemies, vanish; they are temporary and shall be no more seen. The sordor and filths of nature, the sun shall dry up, and the wind exhale. **As when the summer comes from the south; the snow-banks melt, and the face of the earth becomes green before it, so shall the advancing spirit create its ornaments along its path, and carry with it the beauty it visits, and the song which enchants it; it shall draw beautiful faces, warm hearts, wise discourse, and heroic acts, around its way, until evil is no more seen. The kingdom of man over nature, which cometh not with observation,—a dominion such as now is beyond his dream of God,—he shall enter without more wonder than the blind man feels who is gradually restored to perfect sight.'**

As when the summer comes from the south…
Through spiritual advance, evil will be overcome and humanity will attain a higher level than ever imagined, as though a blindness were removed from human awareness.

On this note of exultation, Emerson closes his essay.

Afterword

Ralph Waldo Emerson was born in Boston on May 25, 1803. After graduation from Harvard College, he decided to follow his father and grandfather into the ministry. He attended the Harvard Divinity School and began to be invited as a guest minister at various Unitarian churches. Preaching in Concord, New Hampshire, Emerson met Ellen Tucker, with whom he fell deeply in love. They married in 1829, the same year that Emerson was ordained as pastor of the Second Church of Boston. Ellen died of tuberculosis two years later.

Emerson's sermons gained him a following, and a bond grew with his congregation, but his service as their minister was cut short by his growing impatience with traditional forms. He felt he had to resign the pulpit in 1832. Later that year he sailed, alone, for Europe. His experiences there deepened his appreciation of the art and literature of the Old World, while at the same time exciting him about the prospects of his young native country. By the time he returned home in 1833, something of "my little book on nature" was real to him. He moved to Concord, Massachusetts, the following year, and continued work on the essay, which was his first serious composition beyond the many sermons he had already written. He published *Nature* in September of 1836.

At home and during his travels, Emerson read widely. As a personal document, *Nature* expressed conclusions he had reached by digesting his own experiences and the ideas of many seekers for truth. His exposure to the ideas of others came from books and from conversations with serious-minded friends such as his aunt Mary Moody Emerson, his brother Charles, Thomas Carlyle, and Bronson Alcott.

Nature tells us much about Emerson's reading. Greek mythology, the Bible, and Shakespeare are mentioned repeatedly. Emerson also cites Goethe, Coleridge, Swedenborg, Oegger, De Staël, Michelangelo, Berkley, Sophocles, Plotinus, Milton, and Turgot. His intellectual debt to these Old World writers was large. Writing *Nature*, he wove ideas drawn from many sources into the fabric that became a foundational document of the Transcendentalists.

Greater Boston Transcendentalists met as an informal club, sometimes in Emerson's parlor in Concord. Margaret Fuller, Emerson, and others launched a magazine called *The Dial*, which published the writings by this group and related material. Transcendentalism had no creed. James Eliot Cabot, a friend of Emerson's and an early biographer, wrote:

> When we try to come closer to the secret of Transcendentalism, we are met on all sides by the assertion that it was faith in intuitions; the claim of a direct discernment of the true, the beautiful, and the right. But intuition, with Emerson, means the openness of the human mind to new influx of light and power from the Divine Mind... that nothing in this world is final; that the best must be superseded by a better. The transcendental was whatever lay beyond the stock notions and traditional beliefs.

Emerson wrote and published many essays after *Nature*. He used thoughts and phrases from his journal as the basis for lectures, which he further refined into his essays. He remarried, raised a family, and advocated for causes such as the abolition of slavery. Biographer Lawrence Buell notes that Emerson was America's first public intellectual. In his own time, Emerson was esteemed, both at home and abroad. For people like me, through his journals and his essays, he lives on as a valued, stimulating companion.

Image Notes

Photographs are by Ron McAdow and locations are in Massachusetts unless otherwise noted.

Page iv – Southborough. Page 2 – Sudbury. 3 – Grand Teton Mountains, Wyoming. 4 – Lincoln. 5 – Southborough. 6 – Oxbow National Wildlife Refuge, Harvard. 7 – Charles River, Medway. 8 – Oregon. 9 – Cardinal eggs, Lincoln; Cloud forest, Andes Mountains, Columbia. 10 – Race Point, Provincetown. 11 – Lincoln. 12 – Pickerelweed, Lincoln. 14 – Southborough. 15 – Purple Velvet Coronet, Andes Mountains, Columbia. 16 – Mount Chocorua, New Hampshire. 17 – Joshua Tree National Park, California. 18 – Sudbury River, Southborough. 19 – Bullet Ant, La Selva Biological Station, Costa Rica. 20 – Canyon de Chelly, Arizona. 21 – New York City. 22 – Baxter State Park, Maine; Grand Teton Mountains, Wyoming. 24 – Race Point, Provincetown. 25 – Mount Mansfield, Vermont. 26 – Southborough. 27 – Scotland. 28 – Gabar Goshawk, Tanzania. 29 –Sudbury River, Southborough. 30 – Lindentree Farm, Lincoln. 31 – Cornwall, England. 33 – Simena, Antalya Province, Turkey; Riverside Fishing and Poker Club, Southborough. McAdow (bald, front, left) has played micro-stakes poker with these guys for thirty-seven years. Photo by John Butler. 34 – Madaket Beach, Nantucket. 35 – Sudbury. 36 – Bear Island, Lake Winnipesaukee; Oxbow National Wildlife Refuge, Harvard. 37 – Sally Lightfoot crab and Oyster Catcher, Gardner Bay, Española Island, Galapagos Islands. 38 – Molly McAdow, ashore from canal boat in the village of Cendrecourt, on the Saône River in France. 39 – Ron McAdow and Deborah Costine in backyard production of *A Midsummer Night's Dream*, Lincoln. Photo by John Butler. 40 – Lake Umbagog, New Hampshire. 41 – Mauna Kea summit (13,803 feet), Hawaii. 42 – Southborough. 44 – Southborough. 45 – Old Church, Delfshaven, Netherlands. While visiting Europe, Emerson wrote, "I hope they will carve and paint and inscribe the walls of our churches in New England…Have the men of America never entered these European churches, that they build such mean edifices at home? Art was born in Europe, and will not cross the ocean, I fear." 46 – Ethanael Ni, Madaket Beach, Nantucket. 47 – Raven flying with its shadow, Canyon de Chelly, Arizona. 48 – Lake Umbagog, New Hampshire. 49 – Saffron Finch, Jardin, Columbia.

50 – Schneewind Lab, University of Chicago, Illinois; Galapagos tortoise, Isabela Island, Galapagos, Ecuador. 51 – Andes Mountains, Columbia; Wind River Valley, Wyoming. 52 – Race Point, Provincetown. 53 – Eloise Ni, Nantucket. 54 – Kingman, Arizona. 55 – Slave Market Memorial, Stone Town, Zanzibar. 56 – Queen Anne's Lace, Southborough. 57 – "Peace," Blenheim Palace Rose Garden, Woodstock, Oxfordshire, England. 58 – Lindentree Farm, Lincoln. 62 – Lincoln.

Bibliography

Brooks, Van Wyck. *The Life of Emerson*. E.P. Dutton & Co, 1932.

Buell, Lawrence. *Emerson*. The Belknap Press of Harvard University. Cambridge. 2003.

Buell, Lawrence. Personal communication. 2022.

Cabot, James Eliot. *A Memoir of Ralph Waldo Emerson*. Houghton, Mifflin, and Company, Boston. 1887.

Emerson, Edward Waldo and Waldo Emerson Forbes, Editors. *Journals of Ralph Waldo Emerson with Annotations*. Houghton Mifflin Company. 1909.

Emerson, Ralph Waldo. *Nature*, from *Ralph Waldo Emerson; Selected Essays*, Penguin Books, 1982.

Gordon, Robert C. "Emerson, Evolution, and Transmigration." The Infinity Foundation, 2003.

Green, Tyler. *Emerson's* Nature *and the Artists; Idea As Landscape, Landscape As Idea*. Prestel Verlag, Munich. 2021.

Gross, Robert A. *The Transcendentalists and Their World*. Farrar, Straus, and Giroux, New York. 2021.

Gross, Robert A. Personal communication. 2022.

James, William, *Pragmatism*. Meridian Books, Inc. New York. 1955. (Originally published in 1907.)

Mikics, David, Ed. *The Annotated Emerson; Ralph Waldo Emerson*. The Belnap Press of Harvard University Press. Cambridge, Massachusetts. 2012.

Munk, Linda. *The Trivial Sublime; Theology and American Poetics*. St. Martin's Press, New York. 1992.

Myerson, Joel, Sandra Harbert Petrulionis, and Laura Dassow Walls, Eds, *The Oxford Handbook of Transcentalism*. Oxford University Press, New York. 2010.

Plato, *The Republic of Plato*. Translated by A.D. Lindsay. E.P. Dutton & Co., Inc. New York. 1957.

Porter, Carolyn, "Method and Metaphysics in Emerson's *Nature.*" *Virginia Quarterly Review*, Summer 1979.

Robbins, Paula Ivaska. *The Royal Family of Concord; Samuel, Elizabeth, and Rockwood Hoar and Their Friendship with Ralph Waldo Emerson*. Xlibris, 2003.

Richardson, Robert D. Jr. *Emerson; The Mind on Fire*. University of California Press. 1995.

Twain, Mark. *The Complete Short Stories of Mark Twain*. Doubleday & Company, Inc. Garden City, New York. 1957.

Whitman, Walt. *Leaves of Grass*. Barnes & Noble Books. 1993.

Woelfel, James. " The Beautiful Necessity: Emerson and the Stoic Tradition." *American Journal of Theology & Philosophy* Vol. 32, No. 2 (May 2011).

Ron McAdow's previous non-fiction books are *Concord Village, Imagining the Past at Mount Misery, The Concord, Sudbury, and Assabet Rivers–A Guide to Canoeing, Wildlife, and History, The Charles River–Exploring Nature and History on Foot and by Canoe, New England Timeline,* and, as co-author, *Into the Mountains–the Stories of New England's Most Celebrated Peaks.* His novels are *Ike* and *The Grove of Hollow Trees.* For children, he wrote and illustrated *When you are ready, where could you go?, How Dragons Got Senses,* and *The Thunderstorm and Other Songs for Children.*

PHP

Personal History Press
Lincoln, Massachusetts

Ingram Content Group UK Ltd.
Milton Keynes UK
UKHW050349090323
418218UK00003B/28